The 70 Percent Solution

Improving Your Self by Improving Your Serve

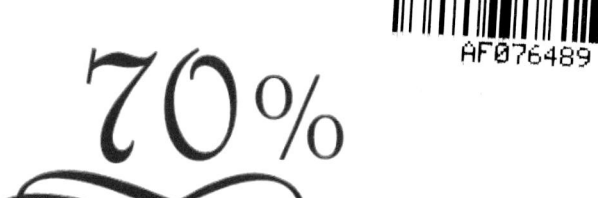

By Chris Byrd

The 70 Percent Solution
Copyright © 2010 – Chris Byrd, all rights reserved
ISBN: **978-0-557-94778-2**
A Lulu Inc. Publication

www.wisdomselling.com

The 70 Percent Solution

Introduction

Part 1	**The 70 Percent Explained**
Chapter 1	My Story
Chapter 2	My Breakthrough
Chapter 3	The Study
Chapter 4	"70"
Chapter 5	Defining the 70 Percent
Chapter 6	Confidence to Become a 70 Percenter
Chapter 7	My Experiences as a 70 Percenter
Chapter 8	The Dreaded 30 Percent?
Chapter 9	Identifying and Living with the 30 Percent
Part 2	**Learning to Implement the 70 Percent Solution**
Chapter 10	Defining "Explaining" and "Relating"
Chapter 11	Connecting "Explaining" and "Relating" to the 70 Percent Solution
Chapter 12	Cautions and Watch-outs
Part 3	**Biblical Wisdom on the 70 Percent Solution**
Chapter 13	Learn from the Wise
Chapter 14	Relevance for Today
Part 4	**The Path Forward**
Chapter 15	Exercises for Success
Chapter 16	Accountability
Prologue	

Introduction

Each of us wants to feel like we have a purpose and a value in this world. We are the only one of us there is, so it makes sense that we are also the most valuable one of us. When we can see our own worth, we can make such a difference with others in the world. We can see that we matter, and can feel the significance that comes from the positive response of others.

Unfortunately, there are people in the world who aren't designed, or who aren't in a point in their own life, to be able to give us a positive response. In many cases, we feel rejected or hurt by others throughout our life that we really wanted to connect with. Perhaps it is a popular person at school, the boy or girl we wish we could date, a parent, or a co-worker or boss. If we let them, this group of people will affect forever our view of ourselves, and we will be unable to see our own value and worth.

I believe there is a solution to this problem. It is by stepping out of our position as receiver and becoming the giver. We win by putting ourselves in the role of the positive responder. I am convinced there is no greater joy than in helping someone else feel better about themselves, and that joy can help us become a believer in ourselves. We become more valuable to the world not because of our status or knowledge or image, but because of our efforts to reach out and support others. We can watch ourselves grow, by watching those we interact with grow as well!

Welcome to the 70 Percent Solution. As an active participant in the crazy world in which we all live together, I have had the opportunity to observe the strengths and weaknesses of people in all walks of life. The strengths are many, but the weaknesses seem to fall into two categories: Character issues, and Belief issues. These two factors will determine our values and behaviors. The purpose of this book is to address behaviors that will hopefully be supportive to growing your character and beliefs.

As a fifty-year-old Sales and Marketing professional, I have spent a great deal of my life either communicating with people or planning for communicating with people. I have also served on various non-profit boards, including one as chairman, and in many other volunteer organizations. I am also a husband, and parent of four beautiful and talented children. Hey, and I have a dog. Not a big one, a little sissy one. You know the kind that yaps all the time at every passing car or jogger. With each of these roles, from husband to dog owner, I have communications obligations, but more importantly, communications opportunities.

Growing up, I found myself too shy and self-defeated to succeed in what I am now able to do daily with confidence. I don't want you to have to endure the same long journey. I believe in you, and I haven't even met you. You took the time to pick up a book about being a better person. That puts you ahead of the majority of the population. Now, the real question is, "Can you believe in yourself?" No, this is not a question related to some new religion about each of us being our own god. It is about whether or not you think that you add value in this world, or if you think that you are not worth the packaging you came in.

As you read this book, the intention is to present an argument that you are of extreme value, and it is most important to your personal success that you believe that. You will meet the 70 Percenters, as well as the 30 Percenters, and understand exactly what this very unscientific analysis means. You will find out that just believing in yourself is not the solution, but is a tool toward the goal. You will be introduced to the 70 Percent Solution, which will give you an action strategy for success on a daily, weekly and lifelong basis. You will see some of the watch-outs and cautions related to going through life with self-confidence and self-worth – specifically in the possible reactions of others.

The sneak peek at the 70 Percent Solution is this: You are going to come in contact with more people each day that will accept you and appreciate you than those who won't. People in general are willing to believe that you are of value, even if they haven't met you yet. If you can believe this yourself, then you can successfully reach out, connect with and relate to almost anyone, knowing that the odds (70:30) are in your favor. As a result, the feedback you receive will keep the positive self-image growing, allowing you to take your eyes even more off yourself, and allow you to be of greater value in the world.

The rewards of reading, studying and implementing this solution are many. You will be able to view others in a way that focuses on them, not on their interaction with you. You will be able to approach difficult situations with a newfound confidence, not necessarily in the outcome, but in your own ability to try. You will find comfort in knowing that not every problem in relationships is yours, and how to deal with these problems when they aren't yours.

Now, here is my caution to you. I am a Christian who believes in the Bible and what it teaches. I have found through years of study that many of the things that we need to know to be successful in life are discussed or modeled in the Bible. I have also found many life experiences related to a belief in Jesus Christ are relevant to daily living whether you believe or not. Therefore, I am not afraid to use the Bible and references to daily Christian living as examples or proof in support of the 70 Percent Solution. You do not have to believe, nor will this book try to convert you. However, if you will give me the grace to presume that the Bible is a book of wisdom, if nothing else, I believe you will benefit from what is says.

Part 1

The 70 Percent Explained

Chapter 1
My Story

See if this story sounds remotely familiar – not about you of course, but someone you might know – remotely. Maybe you heard about them in a story. Certainly not you, right?

I was so very shy as a child that I was afraid of everyone. If anyone made me feel negative, or said something critical of me, I took it very seriously. Even though I was smart and had some strong character traits, I thought that my external appearance, my lack of skills in communication, and my overall shyness were too much to overcome. I was destined to go through life as an outsider, with only a small number of friends, and never be the one everyone wanted to be friends with.

One particular drawback of these feelings was that I was deathly afraid of girls. Once, at a party, I asked a girl to go with me. (Remember that phrase from back in the day?) It lasted all of 5 minutes. I didn't know what to do with it. Another time, I finally got up the nerve to ask the popular girl to dance. The music started, we danced for about a minute and the music stopped. I was too shy to ask her to continue dancing when the music started again. She finally just laughed and walked away. Wow, that is a pitiful story! *So how did this happen at so young an age?*

Well, I could not tell on my own observation who liked me and who did not have time for me. I also began to form in my mind like most young people do, the kinds of people I should want to like. Hey, I wanted the pretty girls and the popular guys to like me. That put me in a position for failure. They were the ones least likely to need or be looking for more friends. Even if they didn't mean to, they were likely to hurt me. I would feel rejected when they didn't respond to me in a positive way if I tried to talk with them or be with them.

I missed out on some good times and some positive reinforcement that could have made me a better, more positive person, with more healthy self-esteem. The problem was in the source I was using. I was looking for all this from people who could not give it to me - the 30 Percent (More on this later).

As I grew older, my problems didn't change, they just moved around. I went off to college, where I had various roles in dorm life, but never really felt I fit in. I would date the same girls for long periods of time because it was easier to keep going in an unhappy relationship than to try to relate to new people I was afraid of.

The biggest damage of my fear of people was the impact on my grades. I never got invited into the study groups. On my engineering senior project I failed, because I was afraid to ask for time in the computer lab. Sure, I had a good number of friends, was on some fun intramural teams, and I was not a total loser. But I only scratched the potential of what I could have been at that time.

To make these friends, I would often need to be more outgoing than I naturally was. I learned how to be silly, obnoxious or brash as needed to "fit in" with the people I wanted to be around. We had social relationships, and did some fun stuff together, but today I don't have a relationship with a single person from college. What a waste of opportunity! I don't want you to experience this, regardless of where you are in your life journey. There is a better way to develop relationships.

Now I don't want you to think that this time in my life was a total failure. I remember a time when my father went to a concert at church and heard a girl sing. He came home and told me about her and said I should call her and ask her for a date. For once, I thought, "She doesn't know me from Adam. She won't know my issues with shyness. I can be something new." So I called her, and asked her out. For some strange reason, she said yes. I only wish I could have learned from that experience. There were people out there who would respond positively to me. However, I remained insecure, even as a young adult.

My unhealthy learning at the time was that I could become "friends" with people by being the life of the party, so to speak. I was able to be Mr. Sarcastic, or be obnoxious or funny at someone else's expense and get a rise out of people. I thought this was progress. However, these were only temporary connections, and they fell by the wayside.

I began work right out of college, and was put into a sales role shortly after joining the company. In my insecurities, I could not see areas where I needed to improve, so I began to think I could be a decent sales rep. However, with my inherent introverted nature, I found myself once again falling into the trap of being the "life of the party" or using an unhealthy method of extroversion. I looked for ways to stand out, most of them negative. One of my friends there told me he would not be surprised to see me killed in a bar as I was so obnoxious I was bound to tick someone off to the point they would just pound me.

The possibility of promotion was not available for a long time, and yet I felt so insecure in this sales role in relation to the people I worked with. I would see other people promoted, some even put over me as manager, and in my lack of self-esteem, I would create a false arrogance that questioned their right to be there. This caused me to have a constant feeling of being walked on. I have carried this feeling with me throughout my working career, and it still raises its ugly head once in a while.

Around this time, I dated and married a wonderful woman. She was shy like me, but with a great ability to make me feel good about myself. During our dating life, we did not spend much time with others socially, so she tolerated my occasional obnoxiousness. However, once we were married and looking for friends, the behavior returned. I did not place enough value or recognize the importance of her role in my life. I continued to try and relate to people with a caustic, sarcastic point of view. It hurt her and almost cost me my marriage. I had two children already at the time, and the loss would have been unimaginable. I didn't see these negative behaviors in myself for a long time.

Fortunately, I had four men who stepped into my life to help me see what I was doing that was dishonoring my wife and family. They helped me recognize that I was valuable to them regardless of my own perceptions, and that I did not need to impress them. I just had to be me, and everything else began to slowly be revealed. The character flaws that brought about the sarcasm had to be dealt with, but the raw material that was me was worth saving and Relating to. They showed me this, and helped me save my marriage.

Chapter 2
My Breakthrough

Sometime after this, I came to a sad realization about me and my life. There was not anyone else out there who could convince me I was of value in this world. Even though I was a Christian, I could not get past my own negative views of myself to accept the price that was paid for me. It seemed like such a waste on a person like me. Did I have thoughts of ending it all? No! I just went into a cave (figuratively speaking) for about two years where I did not even talk to friends, and my relationship with my wife slowly, ever so slowly healed.

You have to understand. We as a human race have this inherent ability to choose. We can impose our will. What this means is that we can at any time make a decision, and if it is in our power to address it, we can do so. For example, I can decide I want a steak tonight, and if I can afford it, and have transportation, I can make this happen.

Now, some decisions are harder than others. Many times we don't even make a decision because we don't think it is within our power to address it. For many years, I wanted to write a book. I never made the decision to do so, because I did not see the time or energy available to do so. Finally, I bit the bullet and committed to do so. It has not been easy but here it is.

With my own issues about value, I knew I needed a change. I first made a decision that I was going to take my focus off me and put it on others. I have always been a bit naïve and simple in the way I view the world, so I am able to give people the benefit of the doubt in questionable situations. For example, when the street person walks up to me and asked for money because the church closed before he could get some food, I gave to him right away. My wife says, "You know he is going to by liquor with that?" I say, "That is not my problem. I gave him the money for the purpose he requested. What he does with it is his business now." The point is, my motives were pure, so the outcome was not as important.

With this philosophy, I began to reach back out to my friends and others I met on a daily basis. I was pleasantly surprised at the response. While there were still a few people out there who did not want to have much to do with me, whether for stature reasons, competitive reasons, personality conflict or character flaw, there seemed to be so many more who responded positively to my efforts. Whether in the store, eating out, at work, with customers, or at church, I began to sense a correlation. The more I reached out, the more others responded positively, and consequently the better feelings I had about myself.

It wasn't that I immediately decided to become self-confident. But I did commit to a process, to an action – to a lifestyle of behavior, which I hoped would be a reflection of, and an impact on my character. Do you know what I learned? I was indeed a valuable person. I saw in my wife's eyes as she was with me and saw me lifting others up, not myself. I saw my role as a father, a friend and a teacher to others, in the context of significance. I began to understand the real meaning of words in the Bible that talked about how we were created in God's image to do good things. There came a point where the person I was in the past began to subordinate to the person I could be. I was able to see what I could be. I became a 70 Percenter.

At that point, my life changed for the better in so many ways.

After years of not seeing myself clearly, I found myself with a new appreciation of life. I discovered that life was not about what others could do for me, but what I could do for others. In doing things for others, I found satisfaction in everyday events that before had seemed so mundane, or even distracting. I was able to create a sense of adventure. I began to understand how I had been made to relate to others in ways that just a few years earlier I would have described as out of my realm of possibilities.

Chapter 3
The Study

Here is the great breakthrough study that opened my eyes to the opportunities ahead of me in life.

This sounds so scientific, but it relies almost completely on the power of testing and observation. There is no statistical significance to the numbers and I might even be off a percent or two. That is not what matters. What is most important is what this means to you and to me.

About eight years ago, I began a project to study those around me with whom I interacted. In every social setting I found myself, I would initiate some sort of connection with the parties around me. This could be in a restaurant, where I would talk to my own servers, those around me serving others, and even the management. If I had to wait, you can be sure I was going to talk to the hostesses at the front. No "get a buzzer and wait" for me. If I were in a retail setting, I would take the time to talk about the products as well as ask the persons helping me how their lives were. If it were in a setting with friends or potential friends, I would start conversations where in the past I would just sit there and listen or wait for an opportunity to add.

In my business roles, I was able to better communicate with my direct reports, as I would initiate discussions as often as possible. With customers or potential customers, I looked for opportunities to get to know them personally, and really see what they were trying to accomplish in their roles. I no longer dreaded going to conferences where we would be talking for days on end with strangers. I actually looked forward to having conversations about anything or everything. I looked for better ways to communicate up in the organization or with other departments.

In my role as a parent, I looked for ways to relate to my children's friends in a non-threatening but valuable way. I tried to get to know them, and if possible their parents. In my role as a husband I set out to be a better communicator first with my wife, and then with her friends, to help grow relationships together. In my Christian service, I began to investigate how I could relate to people about my faith in new and more positive ways.

I loved running into strangers and trying to find a way to relate to them quickly and connect in some way, even if it was for just a moment. This was very challenging. Many people would question the idea of investing so much time talking to strangers. However, these strangers often have hidden needs their friends and family may never discover, but which another stranger such as myself may positively impact.

Over time, it became obvious to me that there was a trend. About 7 out of 10 people I tried to interact with, in some way responded positively. The other three either did not have the time, desire or motivation to communicate with me. Over and over, this number kept coming up. As I would talk to other people about this topic, they would hear that number and easily agree with the implications of this number.

So what does this mean?

In a nutshell, there are two groups of people around you at any one time: those who are ready, willing and able to respond to you, and those who are not. The reasons vary, and change over time, but for the most part these two groups will respond consistently. People don't always remain in one group, and may move situationally, reactively or even by choice. This movement can happen even in the same day, depending on the stresses and situations people find themselves in.

These groups will be called the **70 Percenters** and **30 Percenters** for the remainder of the book. Yes, I realize that Percenters is not a word, but it is as valid as the rest of the science here, so let's just go with it.

As you might imagine from the introduction, our goal would be to become a 70 Percenter, as well as relate to as many other 70 Percenters as possible. Additionally, we want to be able to respond the right way to the 30 Percenters in our life, who are not bad people, just not a perfect match for us. In fact, to another person, they may be a 70 Percenter. Ideally, we also want to learn how to be a 30 Percenter as seldom as possible, and to be careful of the impact on others if and when we are.

So, if you can accept this theory of the 70 Percent, then we can go from here to see what to do with it? OK? Still with me?

Chapter 4
"70"

What is such a big deal about the number "70" as a percentage? Do you remember 70 in school? It was a C at best. Is it really beneficial to think positively about the number 70 when considering relationships?

There are two important things to note, which become the basis for the remainder of this book. First, 70 Percent is more than 50 Percent. Simply put, there is a better chance of a positive response than a negative one. Secondly, 70 Percent is not 100 Percent. This means no matter how hard we try, there will be a group of people that are not ready to connect with us for some reason, at the current time.

As I developed this project, I tried to be consistent with people in my behaviors. My goal was to be able to draw conclusions from their perspective not mine. What I discovered was very encouraging. It wasn't about my self-worth and my perceived value anymore. If I just made an effort, 70 percent of the people I reached out to actually responded positively. Do you realize what this means for you? More than half the people around you are open to some sort of positive connection. It also means that no matter how hard I wanted the 30 percent to relate to me, it wasn't going to happen in that situation. Therefore, trying for 100 percent was a waste of time and energy. However, I could always find more 70 Percenters to relate with if I stopped chasing the 30 Percenters.

Before we go any further, are you willing to consider becoming a 70 Percenter? Are you willing to take your eyes off the way your value has been defined in the past and open yourself up to a new adventure? If you will put others first, you will find that there are so many people out there who need connections with someone. You might be the one from the 70 percent who changes their life for the better. In the process, life will change positively for you as well.

If you are a parent, there is an even greater reason to become and model the 70 Percent. By pursuing this as a goal, in some way you may help your children not feel the same way I felt. How do you help them see that the friends who are meant to be, come from confidently testing all those they are around, not selecting the traits they want and hoping those people want to like them? The risk is high that there will be rejection – as high as 30 Percent! As our kids are able to receive friends and relationships from the 70 percent, rather than seek recklessly after the 30 percent, there is a better chance they will have lasting relationships and feeling more positively about themselves. The 70 Percent will be revealed to them with patience and effort.

If you are a leader of people, such as a sales force, do you see how modeling and training this point of view can help with success in the field? By understanding how to take their eyes off their own image, and focusing on the customer, they can tell if they have a 70 Percent connection, or a 30 Percent connection, and plan accordingly. Does it mean they lose the sale if they are with a 30 Percenter? I would hope not. We will address this later in the book.

For now, let's dig deeper into the definition of the 70 Percent.

Chapter 5
Defining the 70 Percent

The 70 Percent is not a character trait. The 70 Percenters who are willing and able to invest in others are not a fixed group of people. People can go into and out of the 70 Percent state, based on a choice of will. This choice can change in the short-term based on situations, or long-term based on life changes and other factors that internally and externally impact us. People also reactively go into and out of the 70 Percent mentality based on responses they receive.

The 70 Percent are those who are willing to open up to others. To do so is to say that "while I am important, I am more interested in relationships than status." Here are some of the most important characteristics that define the 70 percent.

Self-awareness

It is important to know who you are and who you are not. What are those things that define you? Are you an introvert, or an extrovert? How do you think about things? Do you like to hear the facts up front or do you prefer to hear the whole story so you can put things into perspective. Do you laugh a lot or are you serious? What hurts you and what helps you? What is the best way for a person to relate to you – verbally, with lots of presence, with feelings? Are you sarcastic or caring naturally? Are you naturally open to other people or closed off?

At the end of the book, there is a checklist for you to consider in evaluating yourself. Additionally, there is a page you can copy and give to your friends and family and see what they say about you. Interestingly enough, it is often others who can answer the questions to help you with self-awareness better than you can about yourself. We are notorious for having blind spots when it comes to ourselves regarding our weaknesses, and often even our strengths. Who can you ask that will shoot you straight about who you appear to be to others?

This is a key to helping you become self-aware. For example, I used to think I was a really clever person who added a lot to conversations with my biting wit. However, through my small group, and with guidance from my wife as well, I began to understand that it was sarcasm and not clever at all. In fact my behavior was hurtful to many. By learning this and being willing to accept it as truth, I was able to address the problem. In other cases, I have learned things about myself that I was glad to learn – such as that I am a good boss, a caring friend and a loving father.

To become a 70 Percenter, you have to find a way to like yourself. If you don't think you are worth getting to know better (and you would know) then why would anyone else want to get to know you or relate to you. I have struggled with this off and on for most of my life. I find myself to be a very complicated person, yet I prefer things simple from other people. I end up wondering why people would want to get to know me and deal with all of the complexities involved. I have to embrace this complexity as part of who I am and stop worrying about what other people think.

The point here is that we can always find reasons from ourselves or others to think we are not valuable to others. That is an easy thing to do, and less work than the alternative. We have to believe we are significant. Do you believe? I said: *"DO YOU BELIEVE?"*

Here is another way to look at this question. What do you have to lose by deciding to believe in yourself? Afraid you might let yourself or someone else down? Afraid that people will get to know you and not like you? Well I can tell you these are real possibilities. My research says that as many as 30 percent of the people I try to connect with may meet me and not like me. Is that bad? I don't think so, for this reason. We don't have enough energy to be friends and relate to everyone. Can you imagine if everyone out there liked you and wanted to be with you? Good grief. It would be exhausting!

However, there is a group of people around you who are 70 Percenters due to their openness to belief in themselves. This makes them prime candidates to believe in you. The key for you, then, is to be able to discern between the 70 Percent and the 30 Percent in each situation and be confident in the results of faith in people as you begin to serve them.

Interest

As a 70 Percenter, your focus is on topics of conversation that are relevant and easy for the other person to respond to, whether they are open or closed to communication in general. There are many different ways to learn about what is going on in the world, and a good 70 Percenter will be able to talk at least on a surface level about most of the general topics – sports, news of the day, world events, religion, politics, product attributes, market needs, and the like.

Depending on your life situations day in and day out, you should focus on learning about the range of topics and newsworthy information that would matter in these situations. You would not have to be an expert to be a 70 Percenter, but you do need to be genuine.

Set yourself a goal to at least read the headlines of an online news organization, or watch a little news on the television. Check out the sports pages as well as community interest pages. You will find a wealth of interesting information that can form the basis for connecting sentences and even entire conversations.

Honesty and Trust

People are usually quite perceptive when it comes to evaluating whether someone is blowing smoke when talking about different topics as well as making or delivering on promises. There are natural elements of trust and distrust which come with maturity, job role, family, education, church affiliation, hobbies and appearance. These can be helps or hindrances in relationships.

Therefore, honesty becomes one of the foundations of a 70 Percenter's efforts to succeed in connecting with others. In order for you to effectively relate, and thus be given the opportunity to explain your position or offering at some point, (whether business or personal,) you must be honest. This is more of a character issue than a controllable behavior, and often becomes an area where we can make big mistakes.

When we are around others we want to impress (that might be in the 30 Percent who aren't naturally receptive), we may decide to embellish ourselves either through our actions or through our explanations of ourselves. We may also try to appear like we are

Relating to someone when in fact we feel no connection at all, in the selfish hopes they will want to connect with us anyway.

Remember, connections go both ways with people. If you are not willing to be truthful in a relationship, this 70 Percent Solution is not going to help you. At the end of the book, we will talk about practical things to do with this concept. There we will discuss using accountability to assist you with protecting this critical character issue.

Communication

When you are a 70 Percenter, by definition your efforts are focused outside of yourself. Whether you are an introvert or able to speak to anyone in the world, there is a certain skill to communication for 70 Percenters. Many people are naturally gifted at explaining things in detail, while other people are better at storytelling, relating topics to another person's interests. In Part 2, we will expand on this concept, and see how these skills in communications can be more well-developed.

As we discussed in Interest, you can increase the value of your communication by spending time developing content. Dale Carnegie says you can speak on any subject if you relate it to a personal experience in some way. We all have personal experiences worth sharing, so you have no excuses for not being able to talk about yourself with clarity and interest.

Practice talking to people. Add an extra sentence or two to your interchange with people you meet today. Weather, sports, holidays approaching – it doesn't really matter. Just try it out and keep practicing.

Transparency

Are you open to being approached by others and engaging in conversations that may in some way take you out of your comfort zone? If not, you may have some challenges related to transparency.

It is easy for some people to be "an open book", so to speak, revealing everything about themselves to complete strangers for no apparent reason. We watch these people and think, "Wow, they are way overexposing themselves." Why is it we think we have it right and they have it wrong, because they are so open to share? Is it possible that we should be looking to them as role models of what we should become?

I would assert that according to the rules of the 70 Percenter, we must consider the impact of revealing ourselves as a basis for a real relationship with others. Now, there is a big difference between broadcasting out every little detail about our life and the lives of everyone around us, versus being willing to include in our conversations selected interesting details of our own life.

The ability to be seen in a conversation as not holding back in an area or seeming to be open to deeper topics, more personal topics, is a sign to others of transparency. The opposite would be to give the impression that there are areas which are off-limits, before you even have a chance to develop a relationship of trust.

Perception here is important, because you will not likely share everything about your life, your personality, your products, your company or anything else, until a bond of trust is built between you. However, in order for this bond to begin to form, there needs to be a perception that the bond can indeed form. Otherwise, you fall into the 30 Percenter trap, where all communication stays at the surface, not allowing relationships to flourish.

Consider how open you are willing to be. Set your boundaries as needed, but realize that to risk with others may be the inspiration for them to open up with you.

Faith

Believing in yourself and believing in others is a key part of the 70 Percent Solution. How do we know, though, that we aren't going to fail, or that the other person might let us down, or we might read them wrong and they hurt our feelings. Faith is the belief in something you haven't yet seen or experienced. Faith that is most strong, though, has its basis in other things you have seen or experienced.

This is why faith in other people is so difficult to have, if you have been hurt a lot by those you trusted to be your friends or confidants. The idea that the person you have yet to trust is going to be any better in a relationship than the one that just hurt you is difficult for many to accept. Why would anyone else be better than the ones I expected to treat me right?

Consider the example of a car buying experience. Let's imagine you went into a dealership with an expectation that the products were going to be right for you, and the selling experience was going to be a positive one. You find yourself with a salesperson who is not competent, is pushy, and who sells you a car that is not worth what you paid. As you leave the lot, you have immediate regret over your decision, and sure enough, the car is even worse than you expected.

The next time you need a car, you will certainly not go there and likely wherever you go, you will be distrustful of the cars and the salespeople.

This is another version of prejudice. You find yourself forming opinions about people, situations, locations – even yourself which drive your behaviors. Can you see the destructive impact others can have on our ability to have faith in new relationships? Can you also see the impact you can have on others by your choices on how you relate to them?

Faith, like confidence, then becomes a choice. It is the decision to put aside – not forget, but put to the side- the experiences of the past, and set a level of expectation for this new opportunity. This is faith – the belief in something you have yet to see. Yes, there will be times your faith is tested, or even punished, but in the long run, it will be rewarded with new relationships you might otherwise have passed on.

Faith is contagious as well. When others sense that you believe in them, even though deep inside they think they aren't worthy of this faith, it can alter their view of themselves. Perhaps this action on your part will even give them the confidence to believe in a positive outcome.

Some people say all this believing in people makes me naïve. I would rather say that I have faith in people, and in the long run it will pay off for me.

Initiative

A critical element of the 70 Percent effort is that we are on offense not defense. At all times, we are looking for ways to reach out to others. This must become a lifestyle. The ability to do so is valuable in connecting with those we desire to know better, as well as giving others the opportunity to pursue connecting with us, even though they might not be our preferred interaction.

We cannot sit back and wait for others to come to us and bring us joy. That is not the premise of the 70 Percent Solution. Rather, we get our fulfillment from the reaction of others to our reaching out to them. Imagine a world where everyone sat waiting for someone else to reach out and connect. It would be a world run by 30 Percenters, because they would just move on and do their thing without needing any of us to engage. It would also be a very lonely place, with everyone wondering why no one likes them.

The initiative is the solution. By connecting to others, we are shown our own character. We will develop our self-esteem and confidence further through this initiative.

Is there a time to sit back? Of course! We don't always feel like being a 70 Percenter. Our feelings should not be our master, but sometimes they do get the run of the house, and at these times, we are better off to sit back and regroup. To use a football analogy, we should never be on the sidelines, but perhaps serve as a blocker, making sure that you are critiquing your character, or a decoy receiver, drawing off those who would hurt others into meaningless time distraction.

You can't score if you aren't playing the game though, so get yourself out there.

Chapter 6
The Confidence to be a 70 Percenter

Life is full of challenges, both positive and negative. Each of us will react to these in different ways. Depending on the circumstance we may feel sad, accomplished, remorseful, happy, failed, content – any of a variety of feelings. The commonality among all these emotions is that they are reactionary. They are controlled by the situation at hand. Most of us, if we had the opportunity to choose would select feelings of happiness, contentment, and a sense of accomplishment.

Well that is the secret to the ability to have confidence as a 70 Percenter. You must be able to actively seek the positive in life, rather than waiting for the situation to dictate your feelings. Yes, situations will affect both our feelings and our actions, but from what base-line emotional state?

Hold on a minute – what do I mean by this?

It is an act of the will to decide what your resting state of emotion is going to be. When you wake up in the morning, you have the ability to choose among a wide array of emotions, attitudes and beliefs about the kind of day you are going to have. You have heard about the glass half full and the glass half empty. Optimists and Pessimists have the same view of the same situation, and it can go either way. There is an equal chance of the situation being a good thing or a bad one. If we look at each morning this way, we have an equal chance of a good day or a bad day. My assertion is that is not good enough for me. I want a 70 Percent chance of a good one!

When you realize that 70 Percent of the people you are going to interact with in general are positively inclined to relate to you, there is a confidence that can be the basis for a new life philosophy. Those who come into your life and cause negative feelings or results are going to be off-set in the long run by those who will lift you up.

It is most likely you are going to be successful today in your interactions with people. Because of this, there is no reason not to be confident in the day. This confidence is such a powerful tool, because it pushes directly against the negative base-line feelings you may have – fear, worry, depression, anxiety over things that have not even happened.

This confidence comes from within. It is a decision you make to set your course for success and believe in yourself, as well as trust others to come through – at least 70 Percent of them! I recommend you take some time to journal about whether or not you can muster this confidence each day, and set yourself a goal to try it for a week. The upside of feeling this way so overwhelms the downside view that something might come along to negatively disrupt your day.

The great sports analogy

I am talking to my wife about walking in faith, and I gave her the example of a professional baseball player, coming up to bat. In order to get to this level, a player needs to be able to come to the plate believing that he can hit whatever the pitcher throws. He doesn't know what pitch is coming, but in his mind, he thinks he knows and plans to put the ball in play some way. A pro ballplayer can make millions by hitting safely once out of every three or four times they come to bat. There is a lot going against them though!

The pitcher is focused on getting them out, the umpire may make a bad call, and the fielders are all out there trying to field the ball and get the batter out.

So how does a batter do it? How does this relate to our confidence to try?

First, the batter has practiced over and over again. You have family and friends you can concentrate on having conversations with, trying to ask questions which spur meaningful dialog, and paying attention to general topics that are fun to talk about. Also, pay attention to what is going on around you. Being able to talk about a lot of different topics, even at a shallow level, can get a conversation started into an interesting and deeper subject.

Second, the batter plays real games against real pitchers. Hey, get out there and try. Be confident in yourself. No matter how good you are, you are not going to bat better than 70 Percent, so don't worry. Talk to people - be real, not fake, but believe in your ability to communicate. Be clever but not silly. **GO FOR IT!** And when you have, journal about how it went.

Using the 70 Percent Solution in Sales

Many of my experiences with people have come in the sales arena, which I have been participating in for the last 28 years. Granted, for much of that time I was a scared chicken, with sort of the "you don't want to buy anything from me today, do you?" mentality. I did not have enough self-confidence to think others would want to interact much less be convinced by my presentations.

Nonetheless, I trudged on, and managed to create quite a mask in the sales role. This mask did nothing but make it hard for me, because then I had to add behaviors that matched the confidence and aggressiveness portrayed. These were not healthy behaviors, and my character definitely took a hit.

I had to go back to the basics of character development and get my personal act together prior to having a real change in my sales ability. During that time I was exposed to an excellent sales methodology from Wilson Learning, the Counselor Sales Approach. It helped me deal with the ideas of building trust, positioning to real needs, and supporting my offering. It also gave me some guidance in how to do counseling in general.

I began to flourish a little in the confidence this approach brought, and in my new position found myself directing the sales efforts of an organization as a whole. Once I studied at this approach and the need to transfer it to others, I saw just how different the response was from different people. People who already have excellent rapport with their market might look at this sales process as no real advantage, while those who were new or less comfortable with people may find it to have some real benefit.

Not only that, but I also realized that the method is not 100% foolproof in dealing with all different kinds of people. Therefore, I began to challenge it from the 70:30 rules. I realized that having an understanding of the person on the other side of the table became a tremendous competitive value to me, whether they were a 70 Percenter or a 30 Percenter.

In this role, I also began to understand more fully the communications needs of different kinds of people. It is always an oversimplification to group people, but the 70 Percenters and 30 Percenters was a great place to start.

When you think about customers, there are those that we enjoy selling to, and those who make selling very difficult based on their personalities or approach to the job. Depending on your industry and how competitive it is, the challenges of connecting may become greater, or less an issue.

Most sales courses will tell you that you must find a way to connect with your customer to bridge the trust divide. You need rapport in order to sell them something. You have to develop an understanding of their needs through communication, as well the ability to connect your solutions to the needs they reveal.

This can be a real opportunity for a 70 Percenter. Your natural behavior hopefully becomes one of connecting. You know from this book that in life 70 Percent of the people you talk to are open to Relating. Why would you expect the buyers to be different? Recognize that you won't always connect, but the odds are in your favor. Approach this with confidence and your efforts should be rewarded.

When you gain the experience to tell the difference within your customers, you can also approach the 30 Percenter more effectively. Use some of the tools in Part 2 to communicate effectively and efficiently with them, and take any successes as a bonus.

Time for a change

When you go through significant life changes, you have to take time to look backward as well as forward, in order to really learn anything from them.

You can't just say, "Off to the next thing." You have to say to yourself, "What is it about me that makes me what I am? Is this a point in my life where I need to make a change? Has change been thrust upon me, and do I understand why?"

We often immediately begin looking for things to change about ourselves, which can create a sense of failure to this point. However, if we are as observant of ourselves as we have become looking at the 70 Percent, we can begin to wisely discern the difference between failure and fit.

If we do not fit our current circumstances, we have to look first at the root causes. Is there a problem with my approach, or is there something in my character that affects my behavior in a way that is not compatible with the situation? Is there a goal I cannot accomplish, or is there a leadership style I cannot relate to?

All of these factors can weigh in to a need for a change. However, they are not all bad things. In fact, they may be God's way of direction to a new and different place.

Now, that does not mean that you cannot have faults or issues that will force change upon you. But in the same way the 30 percent can cause us to question our value, change can do the same if we are not wise and careful.

I am experiencing that right now. I find myself with a strange sense of contentment that comes with being released from a responsibility and not feeling guilty about the changes or afraid of what is next. This feeling is the same that comes from being able to release the 30 percent from owning your emotions and confidence. Take a shot at Relating to someone new today and feel the joy of knowing that it is not your failure if there is no connection, just a learning!

Chapter 7
Experiences as a 70 Percenter

How do you fit this concept into your lifestyle in public in a way that is positive, and creates a possible connection with someone who may really need or want the attention? You begin to practice in all areas of your life. That is exactly what I have done these past several years. Here are some examples you may be able to draw upon for your own path forward.

Retail

The 70 Percent solution is a fun experience in the world of retail for many different reasons. This is where you most find people in need of contact and encouragement. However, be aware that your communications efforts here may embarrass your family, even if they know exactly what you are doing. Be careful!

I first experimented with being more assertive in public with restaurant personnel. You know, from the hostess / greeters to the wait-staff, those with whom I am likely to have verbal interchange. It did not matter to me whether they were young or old, male or female, married or single, attractive or plain, I made a plan to speak to them.

In the old days, I would have been more ego-centric, trying to say things that would impress them about me. Things that implied – aren't you glad you have the privilege of serving me today? I would try to be really clever about the décor, the weather, or something else quite impersonal. In general, this was received with a weary smile, and an effort to quickly move me forward to the seat or through the meal.

I was too focused on me to notice that I did not impress the world around me, so to me, any response was a good response. I had to move toward a more healthy view of myself, my limitations and my value to the world and to God. Then I was able to get past the point where everything I said had to bring attention, and I could sincerely invest in them.

I went to get my hair cut today.

The three stylists were working quietly on three women, finishing all of them around the time they started with me and one other guy. I sit down and my stylist asks - So what can I do for you today?

What a great opportunity to safely test as a 70 Percenter!

I said, "A number three on the side, finger cut on the top - leave me some bangs to cover my receding hairline" - then I said, "And make me a little taller, take off about 20 years, and give me some extra energy."

I could have received any of a number of responses from a sarcastic "Ha-ha" to a genuine funny and kidding comeback - and that is what I got! She was so very funny and enjoyable to talk to - has two small kids, loves the toys they have for them now. She loves some strange movies – "Hot Tub Time Machine", "Grease", and "Gone with the Wind".

Now, how many people is she going to share that with? Only those she considers safe. None of the women who were getting their hair cut before me learned any of this. She felt I was a person who was genuinely interested in her. How did I do that? By *actually* being genuine. I *actually* did care about her. It mattered to me about her kids and their toys. Why? Well, why not care about her? There is a great satisfaction in connections, and I received that feeling this day.

Moral of the story: How can we be safe to others? *By being genuine.*

Yes, my comments were silly and juvenile, but they opened up a road to a fun conversation for almost 20 minutes, with both of the other stylists joining in. I had fun and it cost me nothing. And the interesting part is - if she had taken the "don't talk to me" route it would still have cost me nothing. Would have had a quieter cut and a lower tip, but other than that, no biggie!

Faith or Fear? A teachable moment for the youngest!

So today is the big day - my youngest son's first football game. He is playing on the line both ways and loves it in practice. He can take the physical side no problem, but is still learning how to give the big hit. Last night he was quite tired, but got back up after he went to bed to come ask me - "Do you think I am going to do good tomorrow?"

Wow! What an opportunity for me to have a teachable moment. He cares a lot about what I think, and I have come to every practice after work to support him when I could., Every time he makes a good play he gives me a thumbs up and I do back. When he gets hurt, I let him cry, but push him to get back in the game. He is going to be a good football player.

Yet, here it is before the first game, and he is still wondering if I think he is going to do well. Is he afraid? Perhaps. Doubting? Perhaps. Is there anything wrong with feeling this way? I hope not, because I felt the same way that same week in other circumstances.

He was teetering on the faith versus fear border.

It is funny because there is not much difference between the two. Someone I know put it this way: the definition of each of these words is the same - the belief that something you cannot see, is going to happen.

My son cannot see the results of the game tomorrow. Will he approach the game with the attitude of fear – "I believe I am going to fail", or will he go with the attitude of faith – "I believe I am going to do well?" The evidence from his practices says he will do well. However, the things we cannot see but only imagine - these are the things that historically have been our fears, not our builders of faith - especially as children.

As you can imagine, my goal is to have him approach the game with the faith that his hard work and natural abilities will provide him with success. But even if he doesn't have success, the expectation of success is much more fulfilling than the expectation of failure.

It is interesting that this feeling of faith versus fear does not go away for me after all these years. However, I need to be just like my son. Expecting success, expecting a positive response from someone else, is so much better than living in doubt.

A trip to Washington, DC

I had to deal with my feelings of faith and fear on a recent trip. I represented my company on Capitol Hill, where I ended up rubbing elbows with congressmen, chiefs of staff, former professional athletes and directors of various agencies, in support of youth sports.

On the way, I had a 30 Percent moment. I began to doubt myself, and my ability to communicate in a world so different from mine. Surely this world is full of people who won't care to meet me, and who have no interest in meeting me, hearing what I have to say, or dare I say it – m*ight not like me!*

I began to doubt my abilities, and more importantly who I was as a person. I had to pull myself together, and I challenged myself as to whether I really believed this stuff about the 70 Percent Solution and how it can help me be a more effective friend and communicator. I thought back over some of the things I had written, and committed myself to put the principles I had talked about into practice on a new stage.

So I chose, (note - a decision), to go with faith over fear.

I arrive at the first meeting, which is a lunch. I walk into a room with tables full of people I don't know. I see a table with two young gentlemen and a couple, all talking football. None of them were of the same race as me, which has always been a source of doubt for me. Why not try this time though? So I say, "Hey if this table is talking football, this is where I need to be." They invite me to join them, and I end up having a great conversation with two former Washington Redskins players, and a director of a sports organization in Chicago. We had a great lunch and I left with two autographs for my son.

To make a long story short, I had a great visit, was invited to meetings with directors from two agencies in the future, and chatted about children's sports with a congressman from North Carolina who may be a great advocate. I walked around the Senate building and met assistants with the two South Carolina Senators, asked and was invited into several cool briefing rooms in the House building, walked around the capitol by myself, and just felt a peace that I did not expect to have.

Were there some 30 Percent people who acted as if they could care less if I lived or died? Yep! More than a few. If I had approached the meetings with fear, these persons would have potentially robbed me of the joy of my meeting so many interesting people.

I hope I can convey this to my children, and I hope it makes a difference in your life today.

A weekend full of 70 Percenters – My Son's Birthday Trip

My youngest son turned 8, and I decided to take him to Dallas so he could have his first passenger jet ride. He had asked to fly on a big jet for several years. We had been looking for a place where we could have fun (Ranger's game and Six Flags Water Park) and do the hotel and rental car thing.

You should know by now that I have made a commitment to speak to everyone I can. I am constantly in search of those 70 Percenters who respond positively, and who are looking for or are willing to have a pleasant conversation. In most cases, this is not a deep friendship possibility, more likely as passing of ships where each person's life is hopefully a little better from the interchange.

We get up Saturday morning to fly to Dallas. We get to the airport and head up to security. The TSA agents were in a real good mood, and they were very nice to my son - good start! We went upstairs and bought a drink - nice guy behind the counter. I'm feeling good about the morning. We fly to Atlanta, with my son just oohing and aahhing the entire flight. We arrive and I take him to get a pepperoni pizza for breakfast. (Don't get to do that every day.)

We then go to a sky club, where we get some coffee and hot chocolate. People are very courteous and my son is good at responding to people which helps make the time pass more quickly and pleasantly.

We get on the tram to ride to another concourse and there are soldiers on board heading home. Several of them speak to him and wish him a great birthday. *NOTE*: Soldiers can be some of the most positive 70 Percenters, as talking to us can make it feel like home for them if we are kind and ask good questions. My son did and he was rewarded with some cool conversations.

As we are walking down the jet way to the plane for Dallas, I notice the pilot just ahead of us. I tell my son, "There's the pilot". He says, "I want to be a pilot when I grow up." At this, the pilot turns around and says "So you want to be a pilot?" My son says yes.

I tell the pilot this is his first plane trip and it is his birthday. He asks if my son can come with him for a few minutes while I get seated. He takes him to the cockpit where he lets him sit in the pilot seat and work the controls. Such a cool 10 minutes. The pilot didn't have to do that, but he was an obvious 70 Percenter who responded to our friendly conversation. The flight attendants did, too, giving my son a whole can of Coke - "this is what I was wishing for" He said. Oh, the simple pleasures of an 8-year-old. I wonder how many simple pleasures we could provide for people if we tried.

We arrive in Dallas and ride a shuttle to the rental car site. My name is not on the board so I have to go inside. I joke to the clerk, "My name is not on the board because you wanted to know my son's favorite car was a Mustang." She laughed, and said, "Well you have a Camry." I say, "That is a nice car too, and is fine."

She says, "So you don't want the Mustang?"

She gave us the car without an upgrade fee. I thought my son was going to explode with joy when we arrived at the parking space and there was a brand new silver Mustang. He could not believe it. We get inside and it has satellite radio, so he gets two non-stop days of Radio Disney. (Whoopee! Not)

We get to the hotel and the desk clerk is a young guy, by himself behind the counter. He hears it is my son's birthday trip and really makes a big deal out of it. He helps us with directions to the baseball game, checks us in early, and allows us to go to the pool before hours on Sunday. He was just a nice, fun guy who likes to talk about the Rangers, not someone out to see what he can get from us. Guess what – we let him talk about the Rangers as long as he wanted!

The room was awesome - king size bed where we could practice football moves! My son can fall down now and not get hurt-a trick at which I am an expert. We get up at 5 am as he is so excited to start the day. (Me, too. Ha.) The breakfast lady is still putting food out at 6:30, but stops to make my son a waffle. Then we head to the water park, where the crowd is slim - the lifeguards are in good moods and joke with me and him about the difficulty of the rides. Wow, he got such good attention. One lifeguard even rode a ride with us that needed three people. Later that day, a father and daughter asked to ride with us so a four person ride would be more fun. Boy was it ever!

The baseball game that night was awesome - real nice, crazy Rangers fans around us who laughed as he cheered. Hey, their team was in first place and every game was a party for them.

The trip ended so cool for an eight year old. We arrived at the Dallas airport and the sky club personnel bragged about his cowboy hat so much that my son felt like a real Texan. All the while, they were making efforts to move us to an earlier flight.

On the plane, we sat next to a father of three girls, who was from Texas. He was in the radio business, and is a good Christian man who appreciates children. This meant we had lots of things in common to talk about. He was very patient with my son, even when small-bladder-syndrome set in. At the end of the flight, he pulled out a new CD and gave it to him for his birthday. This man did not have to do any of this - he had his movie to watch. But he would take off the headphones and chat up my son frequently enough for him to really enjoy it.

We arrived home at 11:15 pm - exhausted and full of stories. He couldn't wait to tell each story that night and to show his mom the CD -even before he showed her his Ranger's hat.

Most of the time during this trip I initiated the conversations. In all cases, I was looking for a chat, not a privilege. However, the sincerity that is at the base of the 70 Percent Solution paid off for my son.

Thanks, 70 Percenters for a great weekend.

Chapter 8
The Dreaded 30 Percent?

My life has been filled with people who intimidated me, who bossed me around, who just didn't like me. There were also lots of people who I never got to know because there just did not seem to be any connection that would have them wanting to know me or like me.

It is interesting that in writing this, I still connect the actions with emotions. There was always a feeling of loneliness that came when someone rejected me, either intentionally or without even knowing. I would find myself sad or disappointed in the results, and less likely to try with the next person. These feelings did not go away. In fact, I still occasionally have to deal with them, as someone impacts me negatively and I get hurt and resentful, or want to separate myself and be alone.

Here is the problem with these feelings. I was creating them out of information that was likely not true, about actions that were not intended to hurt me. How could a person know that inside I was longing for them to like me? Why would this same person, if their personality is not a fit, force themselves into a behavior that did not reflect their reality, in order to satisfy my needs?

Do you see some warning signs in these questions? I chose the people I wanted to interact with and be important to before I even knew whether they were open to connecting. I was setting myself up for failure, by putting my value on relationships when I had no way of knowing if they would work. I would sit back and wait for them to connect to me, or worse, try and change myself to fit who I thought they would like to be around. Then I created a faulty image that hurt other possible relationships I could have enjoyed with the 70 Percent I was ignoring all around me.

My self-esteem and my confidence both took a big hit from the rejections I felt in my mind. The "fact" that I was not friends with some of the people who were cool at church, or the other people in my classes, or even in my neighborhood, was a constant drain on my view of myself.

I had some very good friends, all through growing up, who were my 70 Percenters, even though I personally did not invest nearly enough in them for what they provided me in time and connection. It always seemed like I was missing out on something. What I was missing out on was the joy that could have been mine by celebrating the friends I had and seeing how many other possible people were out there open to connecting.

I will admit I was shallow selector of people. I wanted those who were more athletic, better looking, smarter, and more popular – all the things the world tells us are valuable, and none of which were particularly valuable parts of my own experiences. However, if I had been mature enough to see them, I would have found great relationships among the "normal", which was the group I was in anyway.

I hope by now you see what is going on here. The 30 Percenters are not bad people. The 30 Percent ideal is merely a behavior that we see in others. We see someone in our life we are unable to talk to or relate to for some reason. They may be in our company, and one of those hard chargers moving up the corporate ladder with no time for a relationship with us. They may be a girl or boy who we are attracted to, but who has no common interests, therefore no reason to connect with us. They may be a family member, a teammate or a fellow church member. We try to talk with them or find a way to fit together, but continually find ourselves feeling uncomfortable with the time spent. In most cases we just give up, and feel like we were not adequate, or worse, that they are arrogant and not worth knowing.

This is so far from the truth. The 30 Percenters in your life are there because we are all so different. Personalities just don't mix all the time, no matter how much we want them to. Sometimes our reputation or behavior creates an opinion that prevents connection. It is not because one of us has a problem; it is just the way life is.

Interestingly enough, every person's 30 Percenters are different. For some of us who are introverted, these could be other people who are also introverted, where there is no one to break the ice or the confidence to proceed with a friendship. For the extroverted, sometimes their 30 Percenters are other extroverts, as each person is so eager to develop the relationship that it becomes a little scary.

Some people are naturally inclined to be 30 Percenters. They have a personality that thrives on knowing the facts first. They want to know about you before they will get to know you personally. They may seem harder, or less approachable. However, to those whom they choose to put the effort, they can be 70 Percenters.

Other people are happy to be 30 Percenters, and choose to behave that way all the time. They don't want to open up, to connect. They like the distance, either for power, comfort or safety. Relationships to them can be a sign of weakness or a distraction, unless they are with other 30 Percenters. These people are often the ones that contribute to our esteem issues, or impact our confidence. We see them as powerful, and yet they won't connect with us. We believe that is our problem, when in fact it was their choice. These are totally different points of view, yet we often assume them to be the same. Do you want someone controlling your esteem through their choices, or do you want to control your own attitudes?

In many cases, the seemingly most desirable people to connect with, the unattainable, are part of the 30 percent. For some reason we get our sense of self-worth from these few people who reject us, instead of the many that are out there to lift us up. As kids we get in our head we are not worth as much as others, because the in-crowd or the cool kids accept these others, but not us. This thinking continues on into our dating relationships, where a failed date can bring us misery instead of learning's, and even into our working career, where we begin to feel inferior to those who get ahead quickly or at our expense, without noting that there are a large number of people we can enjoy every day.

As an adult I would find myself in the middle of a corporate social event. I would try to walk around and speak to the other attendees, but I would invariably find that I could not sustain a conversation with most of the people there. These were middle to upper managers, many of whom had spent years at this company, and who had worked their way up from the ground floor.

So what was wrong with me that I could not develop relationships with them? Hey, I could act silly or arrogant and get a little attention, but that was it. I thought I had a problem that caused me to not fit in. It caused me to really question whether I could ever be a leader. What was wrong with my personality that these guys did not want to invest in me?

After a while I quit trying to relate. I also quit trying to get ahead, as I always found myself in competition with people I now considered myself inferior to. I ended up leaving unfulfilled after finding out that my hard work was for the most part unnoticed in comparison to others.

Perhaps I did have some things wrong with me - some flaws in my character. But as I look back over the time, I realize that these businessmen did not have the time, energy or desire to invest in me because of the need to invest in their own problems and their own desires. It was less about me, and more about their station in life.

Yes, it hurt me at the time, but as I look back, if I had known that it was not a problem with me, I perhaps would have had an easier time Relating. Also, without the self-consciousness that comes from feelings of rejections, I may have actually served a role in helping someone feel more value in that competitive environment.

The bottom line is this - somewhere around 30 Percent of the people you interact have little to no desire at that particular time to form a positive bond with you. Maybe you have some issues, but more likely, they have other things in their life that make this not a good time for relationships.

Before you beat yourself up with the idea that you are not worthy, what if you just decide "I am worth it", and quit worrying about what these folks think. Your self-assurance may open doors to service you never saw before - and the rewards that come with this service!

There is no reason to dread the 30 Percenters. You just need to see your own value independently of them. You must break the bonds of their control over your self-esteem. Then you can successfully serve them as well.

Chapter 9
Identifying and Living with the 30 Percent

The 70 Percent Solution is all about letting your self-esteem and communication values be based on the 70 percent of people who respond to you in a positive manner, rather than having your self-worth be dictated by the 30 Percent who aren't interested in Relating to you, and may not want to communicate at all. While there are many fine people who are not good communicators in the 30 Percent (and we all find ourselves there on occasion), there are some in that group who just make all our lives more difficult.

We don't have to let ourselves be controlled by the 30 Percent, but we do have to live with them. We also must realize that the 30 Percent title is a behavior not a trait. These people that are 30 Percenters to us today might be 70 Percenters tomorrow. Additionally, even though we may not feel a deep connection to them, these people in our lives have wants and needs, hurts and challenges as well as hopefully the overarching human need for companionship. If we can conquer our feelings, and become a true 70 Percenter, we may be able to serve these people in such a way that it changes their life.

In this way, we can live peacefully with the 30 Percenters among us, gaining our benefits from the other relationships we have. We may also experience the satisfaction of knowing we can connect with the 30 Percenters not because we need it, but because we choose to, if they are willing. We are no longer the controlled, but in control of our lives, free to decide how our esteem is formed and maintained. How cool is that.

The Downside of 30 Percent Behavior

There is a certain selfishness that can come about for 30 Percenters over time, when relationships with others are subordinate to their own needs and desires.

Think about this phrase and whether you have ever experienced this feeling: ***"I don't care what happens to the rest of the world (insert person, place or thing here); I am going to get mine!"***

We see this all the time in our culture - from the politicians who do whatever it takes to get re-elected, to the financial people who make a fortune while destroying ours, to the people pushing to remove any semblance of Christianity from our country, to the person next door whose garbage spills in your yard where they leave it for you to clean up.

Our natural inclination is to resent these types of people who are hurting our piece of the world for their own selfish needs. We believe that "our rights" are now somehow being taken advantage of by them, and we can fall into the trap of "getting ours". When we are in the presence of these types of people, we have to realize that they can take us down to their level more easily than we can raise them up to our own unselfish, 70 Percent attitude.

Be careful. It is so easy to become a *ME* person, and this world has enough of those. Finding ways to turn the tide of selfishness is a long-term solution, not something that will change overnight. Our ability to relate to them in ways that model unselfishness, such as that shown by Jesus Christ is crucial here. If we believe He died for us as it says in the Bible, how can we be selfish after this sacrifice?

An Experience with a 30 Percenter

So I am at a baseball with my family and friends from work. We have really good seats. In fact, our kids have moved down to the empty seats on the front rows. In the third inning this stern looking older guy (like my age) comes down to the front row and a bit gruffly tells the kids they are in his seat —he is a season ticket holder. My son moves out so he can sit down as the game continues. The other kids stayed down there beside him.

Later, when some of our group had left, I moved down to the front row and my son moved back there with me. He and his young friends are asking questions like crazy, and I can just imagine that they are getting on this guy's nerves. I just go with the flow, and try to keep them quiet enough not to bother him. A good play happens in the field, and I happen to turn toward him and comment on the play. To my surprise, he responds with an interesting comment. A few minutes later, he says something to me, and a very interesting, but baseball only, conversation ensues.

It was obvious to me that we were not destined to be best friends, but the rest of the night was pleasant enough. It was not a deep conversation, and it was infrequent, but we had enough in common at that point to make it work without effort.

Sometimes we can look for too much from a 30 Percenter, and that becomes a cause of major disappointment when we don't get the response we want (a 70 Percenter behavior from a 30 Percenter). We have to learn to appreciate what is there, and then we can have a basis on which to develop a future friendship or at least some sort of quality relationship.

Looking Ahead

Part 2 will present the communication issues and solutions related to each group of people. From there we can apply to many different areas of our life, with great personal and professional benefit.

Part 2

Learning to Implement The 70 Percent Solution

Introduction to Part 2

Friends are developed through mutually beneficial relationships. If you and I have common interests, common friends, or we just enjoy each other's company, we will possibly develop into friends. Let's say you are a 70 Percenter and want to have more friends. You want to be someone that is liked.

You have two roles in this situation. You have to develop some skills in presenting yourself to possible friends, and you have to know how to search for these people. As a 70 Percenter, you know there are people out in your world judging their self-esteem by how they are received by others. Can you interact with these others in a way that helps them feel like they are valuable? How do you respond to someone else's friend fishing expedition? As we discussed in Part 1, to be the kind of person that helps other value themselves, you have to value yourself. You have to understand that you are wanted as a friend. But even if no one wants you as a friend, you can have the sense of value that comes from a spiritual connection to God.

When you feel this sense of worth about yourself, you can be even more successful developing friendships. You know you have value. Even if the possible friendship doesn't work out, you know that it is their loss, not just yours. You are worth having as a friend even if this particular friendship effort does not materialize. If I could repeat this to you even one more way to help you understand your significance, I would. A 70 Percenter is content independent of relationships, which makes for better relationships. When you run up against a 30 Percenter and there is no depth to the communication, you know why. *They don't have what it takes at the moment- not you!*

But once you have all these realizations, you still have to get out there and do something. There is still the need to interact, not just exist, in order to successfully implement the 70 Percent Solution. You have seen so far in this book that communication is the most important element in the 70 Percent Solution. I want to now introduce two key words which are important to understand for successful communication. **The words are: Explaining and Relating.**

In the next few chapters you will learn more about these words in the context of communication, and apply them specifically to the 70 Percent Solution. These words can have a significant impact on your personal success if you commit to them. I am going to **explain** them so you can **relate** to them. *Get it? Any points for humor? No?*

Chapter 10
Defining "Explaining" and "Relating"

Self-esteem and self-image are keys to confidence, personal growth and success. To be a great communicator, you must have enough confidence to be able to speak with people in many different situations, not all of which are in your preferred comfort zones. Too often, we get discouraged by the response of the 30 Percent of people out there that do not connect with us as we use our natural approach, and miss out on the benefits of relationships with those we could connect with. This book shows how to use the responses of the 70 Percenters to drive your personal success and feelings.

I have been thinking about this 70 Percent Solution, and the solution really is this simple yet complex statement.

Become an EXPLAINER-RELATER.

An **Explainer** is someone who communicates with detail - facts, learning's, etc. They believe if they can adequately communicate with facts, data and compelling arguments, they can convince you of anything.

This is an important feature to have as part of your make-up, because there will be many people in your life who respond well to you when you can provide a convincing position. They have questions and are not looking for feelings, they are looking for facts. Explainers convince the head of a person.

A **Relater** is one who is able to connect through shared interests, interesting styles of communication, and the ability to channel feelings as appropriate into a conversation. This person is able to feel what is going on with other people, and can project feelings in order to convince the heart of others.

This concept of Explainer-Relater is one that I have been investigating in the Bible, as well. It contains so many examples of the 70 Percent Solution modeled, that it makes sense to look there for advice. In Part 3, there is actually a more detailed view of biblical wisdom in this area for your benefit.

Part 2 compares and contrasts Explaining and Relating so you can see where you can improve your approach to others. If you review the definitions of each above, you see that in many ways they are almost polar opposites. As we analyze those people around us, it will become evident that each person has a bent toward one communication style or the other. Watch out, though, because people are most often a mixture of the two. Just like we discussed about 70 Percenters and 30 Percenters in Part 1, people will move from one type to the other, depending on trust level, urgency, type of discussion and other unpredictable situations.

You will also have a natural communication style. You may be more comfortable bringing facts and data to a discussion, having a debate or negotiating, or you may be more relational, looking to connect first, then influence.

This creates a significant challenge in practice, for example, when an Explainer tries to communicate with a Relater. You may have heard the statement - *people don't care about what you say, until they see what you do*. This is the natural position of a Relater, and the Explainer may try to use words which are not heard through the boundaries of feelings. The Relater may not be willing to consider the arguments put forth by the Explainer because they don't feel connected to them in any way.

Conversely, when a Relater tries to communicate with an Explainer, they can get frustrated by a lack of receptivity to the emotional content of the message. The urgency of getting to the bottom line characteristic of many Explainers may cause them to get impatient with the Relater, who is trying to build bridges of trust to convince rather than begin a debate with compelling arguments.

If you are able to embrace and enjoy the self-awareness that comes from recognizing your own style, you will be free to study the typical behaviors and responses among those who are not the same as you. This time of analysis is critical, as you will learn the best of what makes up both Explainers and Relaters. You will also see the significance of the point that Explainers and Relaters are not mutually exclusive. If you have set your goal to become an Explainer-Relater, you will see areas to incorporate into your own communication style.

In this way, you will become: **The 70 Percent Solution.**

Explaining and Relating in a Context

Sometimes it is difficult to learn a new concept, such as Explaining and Relating, without having it applied in some practical way. In the next chapter, we will see some examples of each area of communicating to study by example. For now, I want to include a message I delivered recently to a group of college students which may add some insight. The important theme was that of perspective. When we are considering our communication strategy, (and yes, planning in advance does matter), we must understand that our success is not measured from our output, but the way the message is received. Their current point of view on issues matters as a filter on how our communication is received. Through Explaining and Relating we can discover perspective, and then successfully connect to it.

The Lesson on Perspective

So I taught College Sunday School this week at church. The topic was moral relativism. To begin the lesson, I passed out different kinds of nails to each group of two or three and asked them not to show each other. I told them, "This nail is your truth." After that, I went to the whiteboard and asked each of them to help me draw the nail by describing their own nail.

The discussion was interesting as each had different size heads, lengths, scoring, etc. Finally, one of the exasperated students said, "Depending on our truth, the nail will look very different." *AH HA! She got it!* So the first part of the message was that if everyone has a different truth, there is no one real truth. In this scenario, everyone has their own truth, and each can be entirely different from the others.

After that, I took one nail, and had three different people draw it on the board. Each time they drew a picture of the side view of the nail, I told them it was wrong, but did not tell why. I then showed them the right way to draw it was looking straight at the nail point, basically two concentric circles and a dot for the point. The message from that exercise was that even when we may agree on the truth, it is still viewed and analyzed from our own perspective. This perspective is based on a large number of factors from our experiences and learning as children and adults.

When we are Explaining to others about a topic, whether they are knowledgeable or not, they are going to have a perspective. If it is business, they will have paradigms from their past. If it is beliefs, they will be affected by past learning's as well as opinions in general from their worldview. Perspective will always be a factor our Explaining, as we may find out they are seeing things from a completely different truth, or they may view the same truth from a much different point of view than we do.

This perspective story demonstrates an important reason why Relating is so very important as a partner to Explaining. Relating helps us to discover the perspective of others. This knowledge can reveal whether you are even on the same page as the other person, much less the same sentence. Relating can prevent serious interpersonal barriers from forming as others get protective of their position. Relating can show us when Explaining is not a good idea at the time. *It all works together!*

Chapter 11
Connecting "Explaining" and "Relating" to the 70 Percent Solution

Each day, as a 70 Percenter, you are going to run into a great group of people that are interested and willing to talk to you: at work, at home, at play, socially, at church and so on. You will be able to initiate successful conversations with most of these different people and enjoy the results of these conversations.....***IF!***

The big "IF": …if you are able to hold up your end of the conversation partnership. For those of us who are not natural Relaters, this "IF" is the ability to have an effective conversation. We need the skills to relate through conversation in order to reach the point where we can explain something - taking the relationship deeper. Think back to those first dates with the boys or girls you really wanted to impress. Remember the dates that were successful? The success didn't come from what you knew or what you had - it was what you said. I can remember ruining some great opportunities to develop a dating relationship with a nice girl by just not thinking about what I was saying. Boy was I stupid sometimes! But only back then – not now! Believe me? Well, let's move on, anyway!

Fast forward to the present. After years of trial and error, I now understand the value of the spoken and written word, facial expressions and body language as they all come together to help me relate to other people. Even over the phone I see the values of words, delivery and tone. Each of us has the ability to manage these areas of communication. Just like the idea of practicing as a 70 Percenter, Relating has its own set of practice drills. Pay attention to the words you say today, and watch the reactions of others to each one. Ask for feedback from those you trust on words, tone and facial expressions. People who want you to succeed, like family and friends are almost always willing to provide this helpful support. Begin to see your non-verbal signals as others do and you will make great strides toward effective communications.

Once you accept the existence of the 70 Percenters in your life, you are more willing to take the risks associated with a conversation focused on the other person. You don't need to explain yourself until you relate to them. For the 70 Percent, the ability to effectively **relate** is a precursor to being able to share your points if view, your beliefs and even your faith in many cases. You need to be able to **explain** what you believe not just model it, so that it can be understood in words. You must never lose sight, however, of how much your relational efforts carry equity in delivering your message.

Go try to be a good Relater to a 70 Percenter today!

Chapter 12
Cautions and Watch-outs

Don't Think You can Cop-out and be only a Relater or Explainer!

Each of us has a natural style based on our personality. Those of us that get along well with the 70 Percenters, or who believe we are a 70 Percenter, may think we are more of a Relater. We think we can build relationships with people by just being around them and being ourselves.

Those among us who are more of the 30 Percenters like to have those Explainer conversations, and want to get to the point. "Don't hug me; just make it worth my while to listen to you".

So the cop-out is when we say, *"Hey I am who I am, and you just have to accept that in me. I want people to like me for who I am so I want you just to experience me and think - wow, what a great guy. If I don't match what you like, then that is your problem not mine."*

That is a selfish point of view, when we are designed to reflect our Creator, and He created everyone around us. It is not appropriate for us to be making judgments on relationships based on our own personal preferences, if we have sold out to being a Christian, for example.

As a natural Explainer, I actually had to develop the Relater characteristic. I am full of information and am happy to share it with you. I enjoy people who appreciate data. At this point in my life, I have a pretty decent Bible knowledge, and am happy to share that as well. For the Relater part, I have had to learn how to consider the feelings of the other person much more. This means modifying my communications to be able to take things I consider knowledge and share in a way that is impactful to people who like to learn through Relating. I had to learn how to show my feelings, to just be with people and not have to always teach them something. This behavior is so hard in parenting my kids, for example, when I always believe I have information to make them better citizens, etc.

The same applies to those who see themselves as strong Relaters. "Hey, if I can just walk a mile in your shoes, and we can connect through feelings, then I have done all I need to do." Unfortunately, that is not all there is to relationships. You need to be able to converse intelligently. You need to know about what is going on in the world. You can't just model what you want others to know, you have to be able to explain what you believe.

Relational overload

AAAAHHHHHH! Too many nice people around! I am at a sports conference in Chicago. All around me are representatives from professional sports teams, as well as various non-profits from around the world who are looking for funding sponsors, spokespersons to talk about them in the press, and overall just some good ideas on how to use sports to impact the culture. For the most part, the people who came together have similar presence - very nice, very talkative and interesting Relaters. They all find ways to meet, to share ideas and to get to know each other better.

Remember, I am most likely to be an introvert, but try to stretch myself to talk to those who might be willing to communicate with me. However, there were too many! I found myself closing off, seeing that they could take care of each other without me. It was so easy to back off and just watch. I don't know if I had anything valuable to add, but I certainly had very little motivation to try. The self-motivation needed just sank away with the people all around me getting along so well.

The short question on this is what does a 70 Percenter do in this situation? I don't feel like talking, and everyone is engaged, but there are needs my organization has that can be met by these people. Even though I use this phrase often with my kids and they hate it every time, it applies here. "Sometimes you just have to suck it up and get in the game!" There are times each of us will be intimidated by the Relating going on around us, especially when people are responding so favorably to it. How do we fit into this situation effectively? Consider drawing on your new-found skills as an Explainer. Look for opportunities to provide details needed to give you or your organization credibility. Others may or may not relate to you as a result, but you don't get lost in the noise of the others commanding the floor as Relaters. You may even stand out as different. You get to the point while everyone else is just talking. Remember, other people usually have both traits, and you may find that Explaining is appreciated more than you expected. Regardless, you will live to fight another day!

The Perils of being an Explainer

The challenge of trying to explain something is that most often you would really like to get it right. Now there are exceptions, such as: when your kids ask you a question about how something works and you make up an answer, and they believe you, even though you have no idea what you are saying. *I have never personally done this, but I have heard of people who have.* Or the co-worker who asks you a question about something and you know part of the answer, so you go down that road while inside you are making up the rest of the answer. Or - you may be like the umpire – living your entire existence as "often wrong but never in doubt". *That is often how I live my life. Very dangerous. Ha!*

To be an effective Explainer of anything, you really need to know the basics of what you are talking about. From that point, you can bring in your own stories and opinions about a topic. But, when Explaining something as a credible authority, you are really laying your reputation, as well as the future belief in what you are discussing, on the line when you venture beyond your knowledge into uncharted territory.

When you are asked a question about a topic on you are not an expert, there may be the credible option to redefine the question by personalizing your answer around what you do know. This is a safe back up plan in a lot of circumstances. However, the reality is, you need to know what you are talking about in many circumstances in your life.

The Perils of being an Explainer – Part 2

So this weekend we took my son away to school. He is a freshman and is living on campus less than an hour away from our home. He is a wonderful young man with lots of characteristics to admire. However, planning is not one of his strong suits. Therefore, as his father, I often have had to help him stay on task with the non-fun things in life. I hate it because they are not fun for me either, but I feel like it is my obligation.

Today is the day we bring him up to college. It is a very emotional time for us. We are close to him and have invested a lot into his life. We are going to have to leave him alone, and having graduated a year early he looks a little young to be a college student.

Instead of spending the few hours we were together discussing our feelings and how we can pray for him and be there for him when he needs us, I was all Explainer - Mr. Fact Man. I spent three hours reminding him of details on how to succeed, what to do and what not to do in his dorm, things to think about for class, getting his books, not getting in trouble with the RA's, etc. Some days I am full of details, and I was just pounded them out all over him.

I missed the Relating, because of the Explaining.

He and I both lost out, and I would bet he only remembers 10% of what I shared anyway. Since he probably turned me off halfway through the day, we both missed the value of the Relating I finally got around to at the end.

I hope you can learn from this confession and not miss your own opportunity to relate to your kids.

Sometimes you don't feel like being a 70 Percenter

You know, we all have to deal with feeling bad once in a while. My challenge this last time was a sinus infection, combined with the flulike symptoms of this year's flu shot. *I don't recommend getting the shot when your immune system is under attack. Double whammy!* There is a funny thing about being sick. When we are a 70 Percenter, especially one who is trying to succeed daily in our interactions, we are allowed to be sick and feel bad, but we are not supposed to let the illness affect our Relating to people!

Hey, I am human - I suspect you are also.

If we aren't careful, we will let go of our feelings and we will become a negative, moving us backward instead of forward. You know what is wrong with this? Being a 70 Percenter is not about controlling our emotions and conversations, it is about being sincerely interested in people. Controlling our emotions and conversations means that we are at risk of falling out of control. This puts us in a position of being seen as fake or misrepresenting our interests in this person. Our only hope is to be sincere.

Would the Great Pumpkin come to your pumpkin patch?

If you are trying to be a 70 Percenter and a Relater/Explainer role model for the wrong reasons, everyone will eventually know.

A sincere person can be down. A sincere person can be annoyed with someone else. A sincere person can be forgiven. People see through us quickly. Hey - Care about people. You will never lose, although you might get hurt once in a while. Believe me it is worth it. Then you can feel miserable like I did that day, not want to be around anyone, yet not have to spend the next week apologizing. At least I hope so. *If not, I am sorry!*

Sometimes you don't feel like being a 70 Percenter – Part 2

This is the day I had.

First, we drop our youngest off at school each morning. To enter the parking lot and drop off, cars have to alternate. Of course, there is one woman on a phone, who instead of stopping to let a car in front of her, followed right behind the one in front of her. Good Grief! Doesn't she realize that if everyone did this we would have mass chaos?

Second I pull into McDonalds and even though there are two drive thru's for persons to drive around the building and get in line for, the person in front of me just pulls up and stops with the front of their car between two others in line, expecting to be let in. This also blocked the rest of us from getting into the parking lot. Good Grief! I had to go the wrong way on the parking lot to turn around and get in line. Then I had to let her in since everyone else was so selfish and wouldn't!

Went to work, dealt with slow lunch service and overall a very difficult and challenging day at work. So I had a great plan to overcome this. Our friends got us tickets to a Chris Tomlin concert which is very good time for worship.

They have their normal announcements about no flash or video, and then the concert begins. I discover during the opening act that a solar eclipse was sitting in front of me. This man mountain would stand to worship with the music even when everyone else sat down. If I sat down, he blocked out the entire stage. BUT… at the time, he was worshipping so no big deal, right?

Standing four rows up on the left, there was this short guy. He apparently decided that even though there was a rule about videoing, he was going to hold up his Smartphone over his head (which is why I said he was short) and the brightly lit phone screen was right in my field of view during most of the songs. Good Grief!

I guess you could say I was struggling to get into the music. Then the man in front of me decides that this is such a good concert he needs to take a couple of hundred pictures with his flip phone and email them to all his friends. Then he shows his wife each and every response. *So much for the worshipful experience.* I was so aggravated by circumstances, that I missed a gift from God. This gift was so needed due to hard decisions I had to be part of and people who I cared about.

The enemy won that battle. I have to be more conscious of what is going on and prepare my heart better. If I am yelling at the car in front of me for going too slow, where did that come from? As a 70 Percenter, we are hopefully recharging our batteries daily by the things we do for others. When we take our eyes off them and put them back on ourselves, we run the risk of letting ourselves run out of energy. By now, you should realize that the 70 Percent Solution requires active effort to be successful. We cannot afford days like I let myself experience above, without the self-discipline to refocus. We can also seek others to hold us accountable to our commitment to be a 70 Percenter, and rely on them for support.

Part 3

Biblical Examples of The 70 Percent Solution

Chapter 13
Learn from the Wise

Take a look at the way the Bible records Jesus's ministry, from the eyes of several different writers. If you examine the four gospels, you see different perspectives of the truth. You have Dr. Luke, whose writing gives the impression of a natural Explainer, as he goes to great lengths to capture the details of Jesus ministry. John, on the other hand, seems more of a natural Relater, with a more heartfelt view of Jesus' ministry.

The most prolific writer in the Bible, Paul, is an interesting character. He was a Pharisee, so his training would be as an Explainer. However, his writings show such a blend of feeling and fact that you can literally experience the passion of his message. These books he wrote are a great place to experience Explaining and Relating in written form.

It is my assertion that Jesus Christ was the perfect blend of Explaining and Relating, and He exhibits both of these skills throughout His ministry to both the 30 Percenters and the 70 Percenters of His day.

Here are some examples you can look up and read in depth, which support my assertion.

Delivering the Message to His Followers

There is a story of Jesus talking to a Samaritan woman at her town well. Jesus used facts to help her see that He knew about her. He did not pull any punches in talking to her. He was not about making her feel better, but also not about hurting her feelings. He was presenting a solution for her problems to her. His approach to her created the credibility needed to affect positively her entire town. Sometimes, we may feel like we need to relate to someone because the situation is potentially an emotional one. However, in this story, Jesus chose to get right to the point, to spare the guilt or other negative feelings that could have been aroused. This is a great point to consider when we need to explain a situation to someone who might take it personally. Just get to the point, and then enjoy the outcome.

One of Jesus most significant messages is called the Sermon on the Mount. It combines Relating and Explaining in a very detailed description of life and relationships. He provides detailed instructions on some critical aspects of daily living, and provides motivation in other aspects for striving toward a goal. There are times when we have a lot of information to share. The temptation is just to start a lecture so we can complete the task as quickly as possible. However, this sermon can help us see the value in taking our time, and adding in color to the facts that need to be shared. Jesus didn't rush the points he had to make, which helped His audience leave with a fuller understanding of the message.

He had a diverse group of followers, yet related to each one effectively. He prepared them for ministry by Explaining and demonstrating at a pace they could handle. Because of this, He had to make sure he had enough time to train them right. We need to understand that in developing relationships, there is going to be a pace of progress. We can't expect someone to become our best friend or best customer on day one.

Telling Stories

Many of the audiences for Jesus were very simple people – fishermen, tax collectors, farmers and ranchers. He knew that if they heard a series of details, it might go right over their heads. Therefore, He used parables, stories using the common occupations and behaviors of the day to relate a particular truth. Ironically, the more knowledgeable people of the day often didn't understand these stories. As we look to communicate with others, particularly those who are not as knowledgeable on a subject, stories can be a very effective way to do so. It keeps from having to give out the details, then come right behind and explain them. By painting a picture first, Jesus could then explain his points in perspective.

My pastor gave a sermon yesterday, and he was talking about the story of the Good Samaritan. I began thinking about the example Jesus showed of how to do Explaining in a compelling manner. Yes, you can talk with facts and data, but sometimes stories can be more effective. You use your Relating skills to tell a story that makes a more compelling argument than a fact based explanation

Take a look at this story Jesus told an expert of the law, who came to him with a series of questions to test him. The first question was about inheriting eternal life, which Jesus replied to with the commandments to love God with all his heart mind and soul, and to love his neighbor the same way he loves himself. The guy was trying to prove he was following these commandments so he asked who his neighbor was.

Jesus proceeded to tell a story about a Jewish man walking on the road, who was beaten and robbed by bandits. He was left for dead by the side of the road. Both a priest and a temple assistant walked by but crossed to the other side of the road. However, a Samaritan, who was of a culture despised by the Jews walked by and saw the man. He cleaned his wounds, and took him to an inn, where he paid for his care. Jesus asked them man who acted as a neighbor. The man said, "The one who showed him compassion." The guy could not even say the word Samaritan, but he knew he was busted!

Think about your storytelling ability. Have you ever said, "I can't tell stories?" This point of view is really selling yourself short. You can tell stories about yourself all day long, if you just practice and commit to try. And here is the best part of telling stories. No one can argue your personal story, no matter how many facts they have. You own the story!

Mentoring others

One time, Jesus decided to send out seventy-two of His followers to spread the news about Him. As He sent them out, He told them there were going to be those who accepted them and those who did not. *Perhaps a reference to the 70 Percent?*

He told them not to lose hope due to the ones who rejected him. He also told them to focus on those that accepted them, and to build relationships with them and explain His message to them. For the ones who did not accept them, the visit was going to be brief. He told them not to waste time on them, but to quickly move on.

I think sometimes we get caught up in the long term stress of trying to change the thoughts of those who reject us, and it becomes a stumbling block to us, as we keep a won/lost record. We won't give up. Jesus told these guys to give up fast and move on. He would deal with the consequences. We have to let go sometimes, so we do not miss the opportunities awaiting us among the willing. Does this mean we give up on witnessing to those who mean a lot to us? Of course not, but we cannot let the challenges of the 30 Percent discourage us toward those we can influence. We stay the course because we love them, not because we feel like a failure if we don't persuade them.

Sounds easy, doesn't it? But when we fail with those we love, it can be devastating, can't it? Feel bad if you must, but don't quit! The seventy-two experienced such a joy in their successes that they came back worshiping and praising God!

The 30 Percenters in the Bible

Jesus refused to engage with hypocrites, not wasting His time Explaining to those who only wanted to refute and discredit. Time after time, as the religious leaders of the day tried to get Him into debate, He would refuse. He saw that there was no chance of a relationship, so He did not want to expend energy. In fact, He often made significantly critical comments that deeply offended these leaders. Yet, one of the leaders, Nicodemus, came to Him, and He spent the time needed to help him understand.

Jesus was constantly being challenged by the experts in the law. In one case His authority is questioned. I love His answer. He challenged them on their beliefs, and when they would not answer, neither would He. He knew that they only wanted to try and embarrass Him by "out-knowing" him, and He knew there was no gain by out debating them, so He took a pass.

Jesus was prepared to be in full Explainer mode when He was tempted by Satan in the desert. He was taken into the desert where he fasted, then was tempted by the devil. Now the devil is not going to be convinced or influenced by any arguments. In fact, he was trying to use some compelling arguments to sway Jesus. The

Bible is quick to point out that in this case, Jesus stuck exactly to the script - quoting scripture straight out of the Bible that would have been available at the time, which is the Old Testament today.

I just noticed this - Script - Scripture. Hmm. I wonder if we have lost the significance of the Bible as scripture because we let that become an archaic word, instead of recognizing this is a script for us. In every case where Explaining was needed, it was a script for Jesus. He chose whom He would relate to, whom He would explain to, and who would get neither behavior from Him.

The Script alone was not enough to sway some people, even though He had intimate knowledge of the scriptures and how to explain them. Even though we may know as well, we don't always win when we explain. Pick your battles wisely, but be prepared for opportunities as well. Jesus was prepared to answer any question at any time. He spent three years with his disciples, training them by word and example. Then He empowered them with the Holy Spirit, so that they would have the words to say.

Hey wait a minute - we have His words and example documented for us. We have the Old Testament scriptures that were the basis for many of His instructions, and we have the Holy Spirit. Sometimes I think we won't try to become effective at using scripture because it seems so daunting to be able to learn enough to be an effective Explainer. Jesus recognized this in His disciples. He paced His messaging to them for this reason. He modeled over and over, and repeated the key themes. He showed His disappointment when they did not get it faster at times, but He did not quit on them. He even sent them out to practice many times in His ministry. However, He had a point in time planned where He knew they needed to be on their own.

Chapter 14
Relevance for Today

Each of our children has made a decision to become a Christian. It has been an interesting journey as each child has had a different way of reaching this decision. Our youngest was the most intriguing, and it fits right in with what I have been talking about. He is eight years old and has been talking about wanting to make a decision for a long time. About a year ago, he began to show a serious interest in God and what it means to "ask Jesus into his heart". It was an intellectual pursuit for him for a long time. He knew all the right words to say and was good at answering all the questions about what it meant to become a Christian. He was surrounded by a wonderful group of adults and teenagers who lived lives demonstrating what being a Christian is all about.

However, we really did not give him a chance to do anything at the time, because it was all a head thing. He had some work to do to understand how a relationship with Christ works. Some of the information that was explained to him was actually an impediment, and we had to be very careful not to let him be caught up in an act that would have been meaningless in the greater scheme of things.

Recently, we began to sense in him the maturity of thought to feel what a relationship with Christ is all about. It became more personal and less technical. You could tell the Holy Spirit was working on him and his heart was open to receiving on faith, what he had been so anxious to receive on fact before. It wasn't until the facts got out of the way that he was able to see the relationship and the value of the faith that far exceeded the knowledge. We are so proud and excited that he made this decision, and are confident that it was all him, not something to please us or check off a box - fire insurance so to speak.

Sometimes facts can get in the way of faith. We need to back up and let things move at God's pace. He knows how to work though the spirit to reach those who are stuck on the details and can't feel the spirit move them. Slow and steady wins the race sometimes. Facts are the truth, but without faith they just make us smart. I want to be wise, and that requires faith in what I don't know or understand.

A lifelong challenge

I have a very good friend who lives in England. He is a very intelligent person that I respect greatly. We have had great business discussions, talks about life, etc. He is also an atheist. He was very interested in talking about what I believed, and he could argue for hours refuting what I believed. I found it a great challenge to be able to state my positions with intelligence.

This went on for years, and I realized that although I was Explaining well to him, I was not Relating it to my life in a meaningful way. When I said that he was just going to have to accept that I believed on faith, and that I wished it was something he could believe but it is obviously not, he was perplexed. He could argue with facts, but he couldn't argue with me describing my relationship and faith. It also kept me from the futility of arguing with someone who didn't want to believe.

Being a Compelling Explainer

A friend of mine wrote something that made a lot of sense to me. God is relational. He created us to have a relationship with Him.

Because of sin, that relationship was broken, and life is about restoration. The biggest challenge, since God is so relational, is to communicate that to someone who is facts and data oriented.

I have several friends struggling in that area, but nothing has been more a heartbreak for me that to have my grandfather die in 1993, without revealing a decision of faith. He was a very smart person, and we had a lot of very interesting conversations, where it was obvious he could not relate what I was saying.

On the eve of his colon and bladder cancer surgery in September, 1991, I wrote him a letter, trying to bridge the Explainer-Relater divide that existed in our discussions about faith. In the hope that if someday you find yourself in a similar situation this letter may help, I have retyped it in here. I found it in his important papers when we were cleaning out his desk after he died.

September 3, 1991

Dear Granddad,

I hope you are doing well. Since as you can see above I am writing prior to your surgery, I have no data to tell me otherwise. Caroline is doing just fine, and now can balance herself standing up. It won't be long until those first steps. Enclosed is our latest family portrait. It would be a good picture if they could just get me out of it.

I am very concerned about how you are going to do after this surgery or whatever it is they prescribe. I admire your attitude about having no choice in the matter, but it still concerns me. As your number one grandson, I have really enjoyed these last ten years following your last surgery. I am planning on my son getting to enjoy a little of the same. One of the biggest regrets of my adult life is that you and I cannot spend the quality time we used to spend together when I was in high school and college. Those are some of my best memories, and I get great pleasure out of sharing stories of those times with Kelly.

I am regarded as having some of the most generous grandparents among my peers, and some of them have the nerve to say you spoil me. I really appreciate all you do for me, and my life has been better as a result. I have never had to question your feelings for me and I hope you have never had to question mine.

This is not intended to be a mushy letter, or anything of this nature. However, I have been giving a lot of thought to our conversation back at your house this spring about God. It was very special to me for you to be so honest about your feelings and giving me the opportunity to try to persuade you. Even though I was unequipped to do so, I was happy that you discussed so private an issue with me.

As you reach toward your uncertain future, I would ask you to read very carefully what I have written here, because I want you to be in heaven with me when I am there, and your current views make that unlikely. We do not ever have to discuss this as I feel you were more than generous with our last discussion.

I appreciate the efforts you have put into trying to uncover the truth about God. As you put it, all I had to do was give you evidence and you would believe. I was unable to do so on your terms and did not even do a good job of trying. As I have given further thought to our discussion, it has come to me that God will not allow you to understand Him until you can change your approach. In analyzing the difference between how I can believe and you cannot, even though we are both avid intellectuals, I think it boils down to three areas.

1.   Faith – I think that God asks for this more than you are currently capable of giving. This is the belief that something exists, without physical evidence. Much of what I have read and studied about God demonstrates to me that He does not reveal everything to mere mortal man. I do not think we would be capable of understanding what power it took to create a universe, regardless of what method physicists determine He used. Therefore, we are given small doses of His power, and asked to take all else on faith. However, He does not inhibit man from attaining this knowledge at the pace of technology. Someday this knowledge may be made available to us but I doubt in my or your lifetime.

The Bible was written over a period of three thousand years, by fifty-five different authors, but has remained unchanged during the last two thousand years, according to the recently discovered Dead Sea Scrolls. The Bible serves two purposes. One, it demonstrates the covenant God made with Abraham to bless His people, and how they disobeyed and paid the price. The Old Testament was written to be understood by these people and as a historical perspective on disobedience and the costs. I have no doubt that were it written today, God would allow more explanation of the origin of man, of the flood, and other events of earth's early history that modern man can more fully understand.

The New Testament was written to chronicle God's new covenant, accomplished through coming to earth as a man, dying in the worst manner of the day, and coming back to life enough time after death to be believable, and ascending into heaven. This is the new covenant through which God allows us to overcome the sinful lives we are inclined to, and to attain His glory in eternal life. I believe the Bible ends here for a reason. It has demonstrated to us the results of breaking a covenant, and then it demonstrates His new covenant in a way most understood by people of the day. It allows us to chart our own course, but clearly lays out the consequence of a sinful life, and more so of not believing in His new covenant, Jesus Christ. This can only be taken on faith, as God did not allow for a lot of proof. I can only tell you that I have seen enough evidence of obedience and disobedience to Jesus Christ and the consequences of each to make a believer out of me.

2.   *Hope – this is what makes life worth living to me. I have great hope for the future for myself, my family, and for you. I believe God put me on earth to make a difference and I have the hope that one day I will fulfill my destiny on earth. In addition to my hope here on earth, I also have hope in eternal life: that is life after death. I believe there is a heaven and I know I will go there one day. Even if I was not sure I would hope there would be one. I feel that you have invested 75 great years in this life, and I just cannot believe that it would end with nothing else. If you cannot believe on faith that heaven exists, I wish you could at least hope there is one, and hope that some influence of the Holy Spirit would allow you to believe. I have hope that if you wanted it bad enough, it would happen. This is an emotion that after as many years as you have spent set on your course it would be difficult to attain, and I certainly understand how this has been difficult for you personally.*

3.   *Love – this is the one area that is most difficult for me to address to you. I have always felt a personal love from you to me and I have always felt a very special love toward you. Neither one of us is any good at expressing it to each other verbally, but there is no question that it exists. However, outside of your feelings toward me, I have not sensed this outpouring of love to really anyone else. I know you care about my father, and about Caroline, but since Dottie, I haven't really seen it in you for others.*

You have been through a marriage that really tested your ability to love, and it may have faded over the years into something different. There is no question that you are a compassionate and caring person, and that you like very much a lot of people. But is there anyone now that you feel a special closeness with? I have been blessed with a wonderful family that overwhelms me with these feelings and it makes it easy for me to accept God's love for me, which is demonstrated in the symbol He used of having His son die on the cross. Since I didn't live during that time, I cannot relate to the pain of that type of death, but all I have read indicates it was the most tortuous of the time, or just about any time. I think it was chosen for the purpose of showing the depths of His love, and I feel this depth in my personal relationship with him. I know this is a difficult concept, but if you can think about how you feel when you really love someone, and can accept that God loves you, then you will be on the road to understanding why having His own son die on the cross was so effective in winning people to eternal life.

I know this is underwhelming in giving you the facts and data that would be so effective in convincing you, that to believe in God is the right thing to do. That's just it. The Bible is full of references to how God will make it difficult for the intelligent to understand, so as to underscore the importance of faith. I hope you can understand that what I have said here is in support and acceptance of the difficulty you have had in accepting Christ on faith. I have always loved and admired you, and will always do so, regardless of your belief. My opinion of what it would take for you to believe is a mountain you may not be capable of scaling. Please don't give up trying though, for you never know when something may spark in you to give you peace for the future.

Part 4

The Path Forward

Chapter 15
Exercises for Success

Well you have made it this far. Reading the book is the easy part. It is merely an academic exercise, though, unless you are willing to put it into practice. The improvements in self-esteem and self-worth that come from the 70 Percent Solution are yours for the taking.

However, this is not just something you believe and it comes true.

Success in any endeavor requires commitment and hard work. You must decide as a force of will that you want to do this, to become the solution, not the problem. For as you have seen, the solution is you! When you give up trying to focus on yourself, and start focusing on others, the benefits come back to you multiplied. The true joy, though, comes from not expecting benefits to come, but serving others because you have decided to do so.

There are four areas of commitment that are covered in these exercises.

Give yourself some time!

Most counselors will tell you it takes 30 days to break a habit, by focusing on a new way of behaving. I want this solution to really come alive for you, and to become a way of life. Therefore, our timeframe goal is going to be 70 days. Perhaps a random number, but then again it allows for both straightening out the past, and setting goals for the future.

EXERCISE 1

For this exercise, you are going to need to have some sort of journal. If at all possible, get a journal with at least 70 pages. A few extra won't hurt, as these will give you options for making your own personal notes.

Week 1 – Watch

For the first seven days, you will observe. Watch everyone around you. Don't merely focus on those you find personally appealing, watch everyone. Make mental notes on the following questions, to capture in your journal each day.

Who are the happiest people around you? What can you tell about them that gives any indication as to why they are that way?

Who are the saddest looking people around you? How do they make you feel as you interact with them?

Who has reached out to you today in some way to connect to you? Concentrate on them. Observe the voice inflections, non-verbal communication, words used, facial expressions and conversational efforts of these people. How did they make you feel, as you focused on their intentions?

Who made you feel inferior, hurt your feelings, or just did not put any effort into you today, even though they had the opportunity to do so? What specific behaviors did they have that made you feel that way?

Keep a tally, comparing those who you believe reached out toward you versus those who did not connect with you in any way. *Anywhere close to 70 Percent?*

At the end of week 1, read back through your notes. Underline those observations that help you understand how you want to be.

Week 2 – Start talking

Each day, select at least 10 people that you will extend the conversation beyond normal. This could be wait staff, a neighbor, a retail sales clerk, a person at work you don't know well – just about anyone you would come in contact with during a day, except friends and family.

Observe their reactions, and make notes each day on your journal. How many responded positively, how many did not? What are some interesting things you learned about these people?

At the end of week 2, review your notes. Celebrate your successes.

Week 3 – Explain

Each day, find an opportunity to talk about something in a way that is facts and data oriented. Perhaps it is a lecture to your kids about the perils of walking alone at night. Perhaps it is Explaining a complex business principle, or even a conversation with your spouse. For each opportunity, note your struggles and successes. Try to make the topic each day a bit more complicated than the week before.

To enhance your week 3 experience, consider also continuing your week 2 behaviors, documenting this in your journal as well. If you are also doing Exercise 3, you will already have been increasing your knowledge base of topics.

At the end of week 3, review your Explaining opportunities. Rate yourself on areas you did well, and areas where you need to focus your efforts more on details or knowledge. When rating yourself, you must find seven things you did well for every three you are critical of. This will help keep your critical list short, or force you to give yourself some overdue credit. Be sure to capture this in your journal for future reference.

Week 4 – Relate

Each day, select one person that you want to relate with better than you have before. Initiate a conversation with them, asking them questions about their life. Encourage them to talk, and look for ways to respond in a positive way.

Focus your efforts on being positive about them, while not being negative on yourself. This effort is about keeping the conversation on a feel good level. If you sense that the conversation is not going well, don't continue it. Move on to another person, but be sure to journal what happened.

Week 5 – Initiate the 70 Percent Solution.

Begin actively looking for ways to be an Explainer-Relater. Look for people to serve by lifting them up. As you do, observe yourself as well as the people you are talking to. What is going on based on their verbal and non-verbal communication? Is there a connection? Write down everything. It is important to remind yourself of the new habits you are trying to form.

Initiate your accountability team. You will want them to know where you stand on your 10 week journey, and you will want to give them specific instructions on what to hold you to. The next chapter offers some insight in this area.

Week 6 – Ramp it up

Take a few risks this week. Talk to those people you haven't had the confidence to do so before. Choose ones that because of your past experiences with 30 Percenters you presumed were in that category as well. Use all of your Explainer-Relater skills as an experiment to see if you might have been wrong. See if they do in fact respond positively to your quality conversation. Are they naturally Explainers or Relaters themselves? What conversation skills did you use to connect?

Review your notes from the past several weeks. Highlight any additional learnings. Report to your accountability team.

Week 7 – Choose a 30 Percenter to talk to

For this week, you need to select someone in your life who you are almost certain is a 30 Percenter. Someone you have tried to connect with, but have had little or no success. In your journal, you need to write down in advance some topics of conversation that you believe will be effective with this person. These conversations don't have to be extensive, but they do need to be relevant.

Each day make an effort to connect in some way. Make a note of your progress. Report to your accountability team as to how things are going.

Remember that you are now an Explainer-Relater, so every day you should be using these skills, establishing them as habit.

Journal your progress.

Weeks 8 and 9

For these two weeks, focus on having the 70 Percent Solution become a natural part of your behavior. Have your accountability team observe and feed back to you areas where you look like you are forcing in your efforts as an Explainer-Relater. Make a note in your journal of those times that feel most natural, and those that still feel structured.

Week 10 – Celebrate your Success

You have come so far, and as you approach day 70 you deserve to celebrate. You have made a commitment to the future, by working on your behaviors. You have made a commitment to others by focusing on their needs as a lifestyle. You have put yourself in a position to enjoy a new level of self-esteem and self-worth.

Make notes this week about what you like best about being an Explainer-Relater. What do you see as your biggest challenge moving forward? What can you dream about accomplishing with others as a result of your commitment to this process?

Release your accountability team. It is time for you to take charge of your life completely.

EXERCISE 2

This is a very brief exercise, but it needs to be repeated every day.

You Need Joy. Every day.

Joy is not the same thing as happiness. Happiness is affected by circumstances, while Joy is a way of life. It comes from a series of decisions, and the will to overcome.

I am not a professional counselor, a psychologist or a psychiatrist. I certainly do not have all the answers about how people become depressed or sad or develop low self-esteem. However, I would venture a guess that most of us have had some feelings in these areas. It is so easy to conduct self-examination and find that we fall short in some area. Additionally, the world is more than willing to show us our shortcomings, especially the parts of the world competing for our wallets, or competing to defeat us in some manner.

For the next 70 days, as you are following the schedule in Exercise 1, practice liking yourself! Each day look for something positive in yourself. Sometimes attitude is a force of will. You have to make the decision to believe in you. No one else has the power that you do. Each day, write yourself a note in your journal, encouraging yourself! As you go through your exercises, make a special note when someone reacts positively to an action or comment you made. Note both the reaction and the action or comment you made. Remember these and do them again for someone else.

Choose Joy.

EXERCISE 3

You need to become better informed.

Explaining is a critical part of the 70 Percent Solution, and each of us needs skills in speaking effectively with facts and data. Talking about topics of interest to other people is a great source of connection.

For this exercise, you need to build a repertoire of topics you can discuss in some level of detail. Select from among the following, and commit to develop a list of "things you know". (It is important to realize that not everyone wants to talk about religion or politics, but these are critical areas in which to be well informed if you are actively involved).

- Decisions being made in Washington
- Local community events
- Future weather trends
- Local college activity
- Your church
- The purpose of clubs to which you belong
- The game of golf
- The sports teams doing well in the current sports season
- Tattoos, piercings, etc.
- Current and past fashion
- The latest TV shows

Seems a fairly basic list, doesn't it. Believe it or not, I have had success talking in each of these areas and many others. The list of potential topics is endless. However, there is a temptation to know some and fake others. You will be discovered soon enough if you do try and talk about something about which you know nothing.

Therefore, you need to develop a list of questions that show a sincere interest in learning about a topic that may be important to the person you are communicating with.

How would you dig deeper into a subject? Consider these as a starting point:

How long have you been doing this…?

How does your family feel about this?

What is your favorite part?

How hard is it to do?

Why did you join, select to attend…?

How is it done, played, etc.?

Why is this your favorite artist, musician, etc.?

Note that each question opens the door for them to explain from their personal viewpoint. The goal is not to become an expert in the five or ten minutes you are talking. Rather, it is to show you place value on their interests. This is an important part of Explaining – letting the other person explain.

This exercise will be so valuable, as you become a true Explainer-Relater. Commit to know things.

EXERCISE 4

Become a Story Teller

For this exercise, you will be working to hone your Relater skills. You want to be able to talk with people in a way that evokes a feeling that fits with the communication. To get beyond just being an Explainer, your ability to tell stories will be tested.

What really is story telling? It is painting a picture with words. Helping others see what is not in front of their eyes by the way you use words, movement, expression and tone. A story does not exclude facts, but it goes beyond them to include feelings.

If you ever watch football on TV, there is a play by play announcer, and a color commentator. The color commentator's role is to add perspective and emotion to the facts shared by the play by play announcer. Back in the day, when ballgames were on the radio, the ability to paint the picture of what was happening on the field through words what a magnificent skill.

Each of us can do this. Therefore, this exercise is to prove to you that you are a viable story teller.

You need to select someone in your life to tell stories to. It can be a child, your spouse, a friend – I personally recommend a child. You need to set a time to tell stories to this person. Have them give you three nouns. Without writing anything down, you must make up a story about these three things, the more embellished the better. Practice adding adjectives, plotlines, facial expressions, and other elements to affect the receipt of the story.

After you tell the story, challenge the listener to feed back to you whether or not it was interesting, the best parts of the story, what you did well, what you could improve, and give you a rating for the story.

Repeat this activity as often as possible, observing yourself along the way. Look for evidence that you are becoming more natural as a story teller.

For the second part of this exercise, begin to look for opportunities to tell stories about your life to your spouse or friends. Get them to feed back to you whether or not they enjoyed the story. Keep trying until you feel more natural with the activity.

Finally, look for the opportunity to tell a story about yourself to a stranger. Observe their responses and see if this story helps you connect. Stories about yourself are the ones you should know the best, but be aware that the most interesting parts to you might not be interesting to others. Test and learn.

Stay with this order, moving from one to the other as you feel comfortable with each part. As you progress, the hope is that your Relating skills will benefit.

Chapter 16
Accountability

A professional sports team is generally made up of a group of athletes who are highly compensated because of what they have demonstrated in the past. However, the purpose of the team is not to highlight the individual skills of any one player. The purpose is to win. Therefore, the team will have a coach, whose job is to pull the team together, give them a strategy, and then to call the plays and direct the game.

While the players have to execute, the coach is there to lead. He watches each play, and makes the changes that are needed if the current strategy is not working. The players often get caught up in the moment, and the coach has to step in and redirect the focus on the win, not just the next minute of the game. The recognition for the win or loss goes to the players if they fail to execute, but to the coach if they fail to hold the players accountable to what they are expected to do.

In the same way, to become the 70 Percent Solution is a major strategy change for many of us. As we are caught up in the daily efforts to make this work, we can lose sight of what is most important. When this happens, we are at risk for our feelings to take over and discourage us from continuing. If we get negative feedback, we need someone there to help us put it in context. If we put our success at risk because of character issues, we need someone to be there to help us if we choose to address these issues.

Accountability Team

This group of people needs to be made up of those you trust to give you honest, but gentle feedback. This is a journey, not an event, and you need people that will give you the benefit of the doubt, but still push you to be better.

I suggest you select your spouse or another family member, a close friend or two, and a co-worker if possible. Three people are generally a large enough team. You will want these team members to know you well enough to speak the truth to you.

As you select each person, you should give them a brief explanation of the 70 Percent Solution. Share with them what you want to accomplish in becoming an Explainer-Relater. Let them know that each week you are going to call or meet with them and let them ask you questions about your experiences that week. There are only six questions, but the impact of facing them each week will be significant in your developing the 70 Percent Solution as a lifestyle.

1. What did you intend to accomplish this week?
2. What did you actually accomplish?
3. What did you do particularly well?
4. What was your biggest struggle?
5. How are you progressing as an Explainer-Relater?
6. What do you intend to accomplish next week?

Simple, yes, but their intention is to keep in front of you each week the reality that becoming a 70 Percent Solution is an active effort, not a state of being. Rely on them. Consider using them for your practice on Explaining and Relating. Let them experience your changes personally. In that way, their questions will be even more sincere.

Character

While it is not the intention of this book to deal specifically with character, without it, there is no way for the 70 Percent Solution to work for you. If you are not trustworthy, if you are not honest, if you are not real, then those with whom you hope to connect will see right through your efforts.

Is this lifestyle important enough for you to commit not only to a behavior change, but to a character worthy of Relating to? Each of us has our challenges, and mine are many. However, I know that if I do not stay true to what I believe, others will see this and I will be handicapped in my efforts to connect with them. Each time I have failed, I have had to recover not only my reputation, but my connections as well.

Accountability for character is a much more challenging request for others. For someone to hold you to a standard, they must have the confidence to get in front of you and point out the flaws your own blinders keep you from seeing. I encourage you to investigate a group of people your same gender that you can trust to hold you to this standard, without fear of your reaction. In my life I have experienced the great value of this support, and I would not be where I am today without them.

Are you a 70 Percenter?

Use this table to rate yourself, and give copies to your accountability group and others you trust to give you honest feed-back about where you stand. You might consider doing this in week 1, with one group of people, and week 10 with another group.

Characteristic	How I rate myself - How others rate me
Self-Awareness – Do I have a good real picture in my mind of who I am, and as others see me?	
Interest – Do I demonstrate to others that I care about what they are communicating?	
Honesty and Trust – Do I represent myself truthfully and honestly to others?	
Communication – Do I work hard to have value in my side of a conversation?	
Transparency – Do others see the real me, or do I hide myself from them?	
Faith – Do I demonstrate that I believe in myself and others?	
Initiative – Do I look for ways to reach out to others?	

Prologue

Congratulations! You have invested in learning about a method for increasing your self-esteem and your self-worth, by committing to serve others. This speaks highly of you and your interest in bettering yourself.

Whether you were looking for a few good ideas to add to an already fulfilling life, or were looking for a total communications makeover, I hope that something in this book has been of value to you. There is a great need in our culture for people to reach out and serve others. Discovering that we can see our own value, not by selfish actions, but by investing in others, means we can benefit ourselves through benefitting others. What a life changing concept. It releases us to serve, and allows us to experience true joy in our lives.

Remember, 70 Percent of the people who you come in contact with have a positive view of relationships and are open to communications that might reveal a common interest. However, you must actively reach out. Don't wait on anyone else. You be the action owner. As you go, don't let the 30 Percenters steal your joy. Remember, if there is no connection, it is not a reflection of your qualities.

Take your first steps today with confidence, knowing that others have been there before you, wanting to change for the better and be a light to others by becoming a 70 Percent Solution.

www.ingramcontent.com/pod-product-compliance
Ingram Content Group UK Ltd.
Pitfield, Milton Keynes, MK11 3LW, UK
UKHW041958230426
12048UKWH00008B/397